LEEDS IN 50 BUILDINGS

PAUL CHRYSTAL

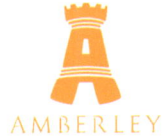

Map contains Ordnance Survey data © Crown copyright and database right [2016]

This edition first published 2016

Amberley Publishing, The Hill, Stroud
Gloucestershire GL5 4EP

www.amberley-books.com

Copyright © Paul Chrystal, 2016

The right of Paul Chrystal to be identified as the Author of this work has been asserted in accordance with the Copyrights, Designs and Patents Act 1988.

All rights reserved. No part of this book may be reprinted or reproduced or utilised in any form or by any electronic, mechanical or other means, now known or hereafter invented, including photocopying and recording, or in any information storage or retrieval system, without the permission in writing from the Publishers.

British Library Cataloguing in Publication Data.
A catalogue record for this book is available from the British Library.

ISBN 978 1 4456 5454 6 (print)
ISBN 978 1 4456 5455 3 (ebook)

Typesetting and Origination by Amberley Publishing.
Printed in Great Britain.

Appointed GPSR EU Representative: Easy Access System Europe Oü, 16879218
Address: Mustamäe tee 50, 10621, Tallinn, Estonia
Contact Details: gpsr.requests@easproject.com, +358 40 500 3575

Contents

Preface	4
Map	5
Introduction	6
The 50 Buildings	17
A Leeds Building Timeline	92
Websites	95
Acknowledgements	96

Preface

Buildings are one of the crucial features which define a city. Prominent buildings create the cityscape and form the horizon; at a different, more personal level, they provide the homes and work for that city's citizens, their places of education, worship, entertainment, the arts and commerce.

The fifty buildings described and depicted here chart the history of Leeds from its pivotal role in the Industrial Revolution as a major producer of wool and white broadcloth at the third White Cloth Hall (1775), the 1792 flax-spinning Marshall's Mill and the stunning corn exchange (1863). Armley Mills, Midland Mill and Temple Works complete the old industrial picture. For education, Leeds boasts four universities, with the Brotherton Library of Leeds University taking pride of place, and the Rosebowl Building at Leeds Beckett. The Thackray museum of medical history, the city museum, Armley Mills and the armouries are inspiring inside and out and provide cutting-edge culture and entertainment along with the Art Gallery, the Grand Theatre, City Varieties, Hyde Park Picture House, the West Yorkshire Playhouse and the new Leeds Arena. Civic grandeur, much but not all of it Victorian, is represented by the market halls, City Square, the town hall and later, the civic hall. For sport there is Headingly and Elland Road while the beautifully elegant corn exchange and the Victorian arcades provide a very special shopping experience. The skyline is now pierced with twenty-first-century 'scrapers, not least windy Bridgewater Place, Candle House, Sky Plaza and the bronze Broadcasting Tower. Churches and mosques abound, as do venerable old pubs like Whitelocks.

All of these buildings and many more are covered in this fascinating book: their history and the role they play today in one of England's leading cities provide an enthralling historical narrative for the Leeds of yesterday and of today.

Space permits the inclusion of only fifty buildings – the book could easily have been twice the extent covering 100-or-so buildings. The fifty included are listed chronologically.

Paul Chrystal,
January 2016

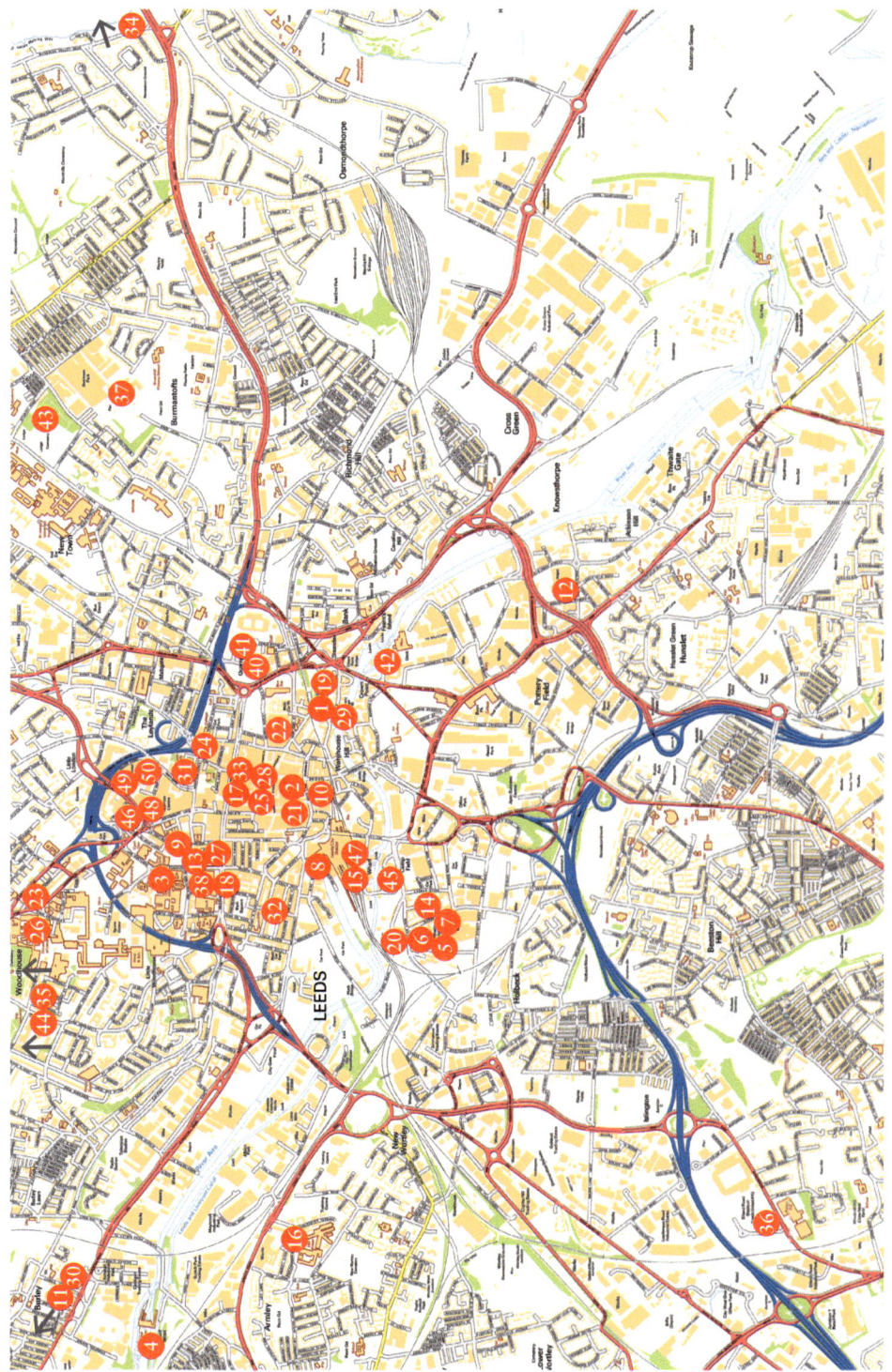

Introduction

The first mention of the name 'Leeds' comes from Bede's *Historia Ecclesiastica*, published in around AD 731, when he talks about a church altar built by Edwin of Northumbria in 'the region known as Loidis'. This altar was Leeds' first-known building. That area of ancient Britain was Welsh speaking and resistant to the Anglo-Saxons. It was a subdivision of Elmet, which was also a Welsh speaking area that was later a part of the Kingdom of Northumbria. Ledston and Ledsham, both situated nearby, were also part of Loidis and are reflected in its name, a name which may be the name of a tribe meaning 'people of the flowing river' – the river being the Aire on which Leeds stands and on which it has always depended.

We learn from an eleventh-century manuscript that in the tenth century, Loidis lay on the boundary between the Viking kingdom of Jorvik and the Welsh-speaking Kingdom of Strathclyde – Lancashire, Cumbria and south-western Scotland. Pen-y-Ghent, Craven, Hatfield, Aldborough and Stanwick provide more evidence of the Welsh influence.

The name crops up again in the 1086 Domesday Book describing a settlement in Old English as Ledes. It tells us that Ledes has 'a priest, a church, a mill and ten acres of meadow, twenty-seven labourers, four freemen and four cottagers'. From the 1862 *Annals of Yorkshire* we learn that,

> in excavating for the foundations of the warehouses on the south side of West Bar, in 1836, the workmen discovered the remains of the Castle Moat. It appeared to have had a semicircular form, and to have terminated in the Mill Goite, extending considerably on each side of Scarborough's Hotel, on which site the castle is supposed to have stood. A tower also stood near Lydgate in Woodhouse Lane, called Tower Hill; which was probably connected with the castle; but not a vestige of either fabric remains.

An inhabitant of Leeds is still known locally as a Loiner, a word which could be derived from Loidis. In medieval times Loidis was Leedis, from which the modern name of the city derives.

The discovery in 2009 of the West Yorkshire hoard from the eleventh century suggests the existence of an affluent Anglo-Saxon settlement comprising largely of an ecclesiastical site, a ford over the Aire, and what is now Kirkgate. After the conquest, Leeds was spared the devastation and depredation that was the fate of many settlements in the vengeful Harrying of the North by William I, however

Seacroft, Garforth, Coldcotes, Manston, Bramley, Beeston, Halton, and Allerton were comprehensively laid to waste.

In 1086 Leeds had a population of at least 200. The settlement was clustered on land around the parish church, and the manor house some half a mile to the west. Apart from the evidence from *The Annals of Yorkshire* mentioned above, we know from *The Leeds Guide* of 1837 that Ilbert de Lacy built a castle around 1080 on Mill Hill – today's City Square – besieged by Stephen on his way to Scotland in 1139. Leeds Castle occupied the site surrounded in 1862 by Mill Hill, Bishopgate, and the western part of Boar Lane. It was probably encircled by a moat and an extensive park as evidenced by the names Park Row and Park Square. According to the *Hardynge Chronicle* in 1399, Richard II was imprisoned at Leeds before being moved to Pontefract, where he was executed.

The parish church was the premier ecclesiastical building but there were also many chantry chapels around Briggate and Kirkgate. A famous mid-twelfth-century Norman church can still be seen at Adel; at Whitkirk the church is the only medieval church within the old city boundaries.

Kirkstall Abbey was founded in 1152 by Henry Lacy in woodland next to the River Aire 3 miles northwest of Leeds village. It was a Cistercian foundation originating from Fountains Abbey and, like Rievaulx, Jervaulx and Fountains, became a powerful landowner, developing industries like iron forging, but more significantly for the emergent Leeds, wool-making. Kirkstall Abbey is said to have owned around 5,000 sheep at one time.

In 1207 Leeds received its first charter, which led to a new town being laid out along one street overseen by the Lord of the Manor, Maurice de Gant. This was Brigg Gata, later to be called Briggate, and was wide enough to support a bustling market; the earliest recorded bridge (Briggate comes from *brycg*, Old English for bridge and gata, Old Norse for a way or a street), is in 1384. Headrow gets its name from the heads of executed criminals placed here all in in a row. The population was small in 1207 and remained so for a long time afterwards. The Poll Tax of 1379 reveals that the population was less than 300 then, making Leeds one of the smallest towns in Yorkshire – Snaith, Ripon, Tickhill, and Selby were all larger.

In the later Middle Ages, Leeds remained devoid of military or commercial significance, although this may have been the time when it saw the birth and rise of its weaving and wool trade – pioneered locally by the Cistercians at Kirkstall Abbey. Agriculture was still very much the name of the game. Early Leeds streets would be narrow, muddy and dark. The houses were of wood, whitewashed, and often thatched. However, by the fourteenth century Leeds was starting to develop. There were two innkeepers, a butcher, and three smiths working here. The genesis of the textile trade is indicated by the three dye vats in Kirkgate, then there was the common oven where bread was baked. The manor house stood to the west of the town, where the Scarbrough Hotel is now. Park Row, Park Place and Park Square show us the extent of the royal hunting grounds and Basinghall Street, formerly Butts Lane, was the site of the archery butts. Grain fields flourished at

Burmantofts, the borough men's tofts, ground into flour at the watermill at the bottom of Mill Hill. Ralph Thoresby in his famous *Topographical Survey of the Parish of Leeds*, published in 1715, tells us that the cloth was routinely laid out on the battlements of the bridge, and on benches below, every Tuesday and Saturday morning.

It was the Tudors who saw Leeds become an established cloth-trading town, although in 1470 it was still obscure enough to be described somewhat dismissively as being 'near to Rothwell' then a modest market town. In 1536 the traveller and poet John Leland visited and described it as

> Two miles lower than Christal [Kirkstall] Abbey, on Aire River, a praty [pretty] market town which stondith most by clothing having one paroche churche reasonably well buildid and was as large as Bradford, though not so quik.

'Not so quik' meaning not as commercially sharp.

Education first makes its mark in Leeds in 1552, when William Sheafield, a chantry priest of St Catherine in Leeds, left provision for a 'learned school-master who should teach freely for ever such scholars, youths, and children as should resort to him, with the wise proviso that the Leeds folk themselves should find a suitable building and make up the master's salary to ten pounds a year'. So Leeds Grammar School was born, first located in The Calls, and later in Lady Lane. In 1626, Leeds was granted its first charter of incorporation from Charles I, which presumed that Leeds was 'an ancient and populous town, whose inhabitants are well acquainted with the art and mystery of making Woollen Cloths'. The aim in requesting the charter was to put an end to the shoddy work that was being turned out in other towns at the expense of Leeds' hard-won reputation. John Harrison, a Leeds woollen merchant and benefactor, was a champion of this cause: he built St John's church at the top of Briggate in 1634 and replaced the old grammar school in 1642.

The fearless and adventurous Celia Fiennes called in at Leeds and, although she seems more preoccupied with the price and strength of beer and whether her cheese sandwich should be on the house or not, she does give us a contemporary picture of the town in her 1698 *Through England On a Side Saddle in the Time of William and Mary*:

> Leeds is a Large town, severall Large streetes, Cleane and well pitch'd and good houses all built of stone. Some have good Gardens and Steps up to their houses and walls before them. This is Esteemed the Wealthyest town of its bigness in the Country its manufacture is ye woollen Cloth – the Yorkshire Cloth in wch they are all Employ'd and are Esteemed very Rich and very proud. They have provision soe plentiful yt they may Live wth very Little Expense and get much variety; here if one Calls for a tankard of Ale wch is allwayes a groate it's the only dear thing all over Yorkshire, their ale is very strong … but for paying this Groat for your ale you may have a slice of meate Either hott or Cold according to the tyme of day

you Call, or Else butter and Cheese Gratis into the bargaine; this was a Generall Custom in most parts of Yorkshire but now they have almost Changed it, and tho' they still retaine the great price for the ale, yet Make strangers pay for their meate, and at some places at great rates, notwithstanding how Cheape they have all their provision. There is still this Custome on a Market day at Leeds, the sign of ye bush just by the Bridge, anybody yt will goe and Call for one tanchard of ale and a pinte of wine and pay for these only shall be set to a table to Eate wth two or three dishes of good meate and a dish of sweetmeates after. Had I known this and ye Day wch was their Market I would have Come then but I happened to Come a day after ye market, however I did only pay for three tankards of ale and wt I Eate, and my servants was gratis. This town is full of discenters, there are two Large meeting places, here is also a good schoole for young Gentlewomen; the streetes are very broad, the Market Large.

A few years later Daniel Defoe, in his *A Tour Through the Whole Island of Great Britain*, agrees – although he is not so obsessed with the beer and bar meals on offer and provides a meticulously detailed description of the Leeds wool trade, abbreviated here:

Leeds is a large, wealthy and populous town, it stands on the north bank of the River Aire, or rather on both sides the river, for there is a large suburb or part of the town on the south side of the river, and the whole is joined by a stately and prodigiously strong stone bridge, so large, and so wide, that formerly the cloth market was kept in neither part of the town, but on the very bridge itself; and therefore the refreshment given the clothiers by the inn-keepers, of which I shall speak presently is called the Brigg-shot to this day.

The encrease of the manufacturers and of the trade, soon made the market too great to be confined to the brigg or bridge, and it is now kept in the High-street, beginning from the bridge, and running up north almost to the market-house, where the ordinary market for provisions begins, which also is the greatest of its kind in all the north of England, except Hallifax ... The street is a large, broad, fair, and well-built street, beginning, as I have said, at the bridge, and ascending gently to the north ... The town of Leeds is very large, and, as above, there are abundance of wealthy merchants in it. Here are two churches, and two large meeting-houses of dissenters, and six or seven chapels of ease, besides dissenter's chapels, in the adjacent, depending villages.

Home trade was important:

There are for this purpose a set of travelling merchants in Leeds, who go all over England with droves of pack horses, and to all the fairs and market towns over the whole island ... they supply the shops by wholesale or whole pieces; and not only so, but give large credit too ...; 'tis ordinary for one of these men to carry a thousand pounds value of cloth with them at a time'.

But export more so:

> Warehouse-keepers not only supply all the shop-keepers and wholesale men in London, but sell also very great quantities to the merchants, as well for exportation to the English colonies … especially New England, New York, Virginia, and as also to the Russia merchants, who send an exceeding quantity to Petersburgh, Riga, Dantzic, Narva, and to Sweden and Pomerania.

Then there are

> the merchants, that is to say, such as receive commissions from abroad to buy cloth for the merchants chiefly in Hamburgh, and in Holland, and from several other parts; and these are not only many in number, but some of them are very considerable in their dealings, and correspond as far as Nuremberg, Frankfort, Leipsick, and even to Vienna and Ausburgh, in the farthest provinces of Germany.

Around the same time Ralph Thoresby, the Samuel Pepys of the North, kept a diary and published, among other works, his famous *Ducatus Leodiensis*, the first history of Leeds. The city's historical society, formed in 1889, was named after him. By the early eighteenth century Leeds was largely a mercantile town. The population exploded from 10,000 at the end of the seventeenth century to 30,000 at the end of the eighteenth. In the 1770s Leeds merchants contributed 30 per cent of the country's woollen exports, valued at £1,500,000; seventy years previously the whole of Yorkshire accounted for only 20 per cent of the nation's exports.

Leeds and places to the west of Leeds specialised in the making of 'Northern Dozens' or 'Yorkshire Broadcloths' – inexpensive, good-quality cloths. Cloth and textiles defined Leeds: the wealth that it brought shaped the city in every way, not least the buildings which were constructed to manufacture, market and distribute the finished goods. We have noted how the Cistercians at Kirkstall were very active in sheep farming. Perhaps the earliest reference to cloth-making in Leeds was in 1275 but in 1201 we hear of Simon the Dyer, who was convicted of selling adulterated wine. Leland describes the cloth market on the bridge over the Aire at the bottom of Briggate at specified times and under specific conditions. This woollen cloth was predominantly made at homes in Leeds and in the villages around Leeds. There was a fulling mill in Leeds by 1400, and cloth dying was also established. The trade in cloth soon exceeded the capacity at the bridge, and was transferred to trestle tables in two rows on either side of Briggate. Defoe, as we have seen, notes that Leeds traders went all over the country, selling their cloth on credit, and that a lively export trade existed. By the end of the seventeenth century, the cloth market was held on Tuesdays and Saturdays on Leeds Bridge.

Thoresby established the first covered cloth market: the White Cloth Hall, which opened on 22 May 1711 behind the corn exchange, and traded here for sixty-five years before moving to a new site in The Calls. In 1758 the Coloured

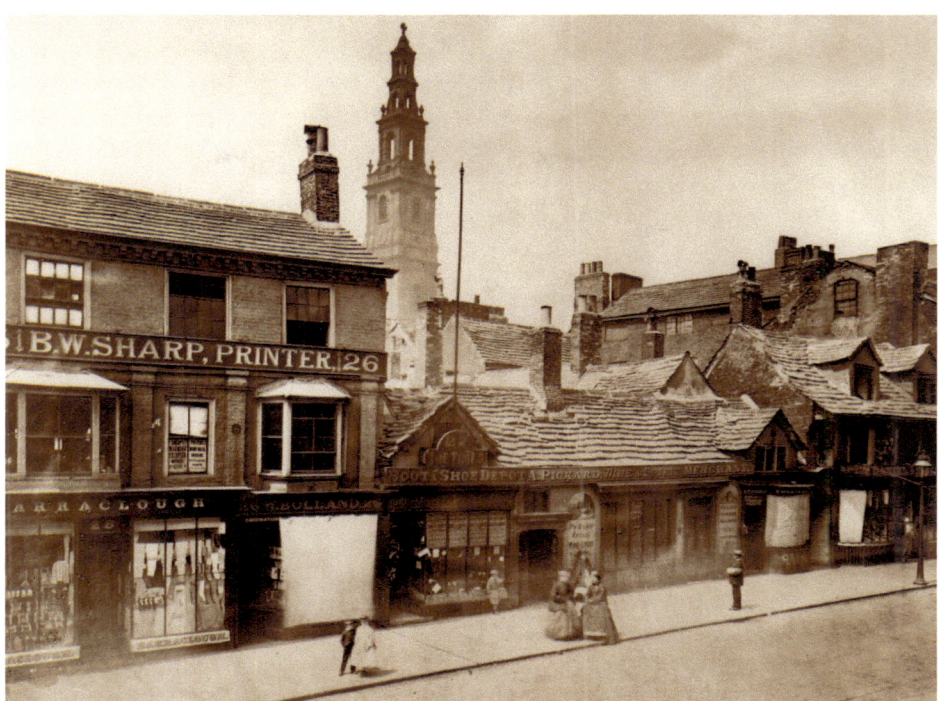

Sixteenth-century buildings in Lower Briggate. On the left at No. 25 is hosier John Barraclough on the ground floor and B. W. Sharp, printers, above that, addressed as No. 26. Below, also at No. 26, is William Bolland, bookseller. In the late 1860s clockmakers and jewellers John Dyson & Son moved from The Calls to No. 24 Briggate, eventually expanding to Nos 25 and 26: the Time Ball Buildings. You can also see the boot and shoe depot run by James Lowley at No. 27 and *The Times* advert above The Golden Fleece pub (No. 28) run by wine and spirit merchant, Anthony Pickard. Miss Julia Pickard ran the tobacconist at No. 29 and Daniel Pickard & Co., the linen drapers, at No. 30. It is likely that these buildings were demolished not long after this photograph was taken when Boar Lane was widened in 1867. The spire of Trinity church is visible in the centre background. (Photograph by Wormald of Leeds. Courtesy of Leodis – a photographic archive of Leeds; © Leeds Library & Information Services)

Cloth Hall, or Mixed Cloth Hall, was built near Mill Hill for the sale of dyed cloth, capacious enough for 1800 trading stalls, initially let at 3 guineas per annum, but later trading at a premium of £24 per annum. The hall was demolished in 1899 to make way for the new general post office; the last White Cloth Hall met its end in 1896 to allow for the Metropole Hotel.

There were, of course, other industries. Leeds pottery was founded in 1770 and there was brick-making, coach-makers, clockmakers, booksellers and jewellers. The first newspaper in Leeds went to press in 1718. Over the years flax, cotton, silk, off-the-peg clothing at Burton's and others, engineering, locomotives, carpets, brewing at Tetley's from 1822 and at Kirkstall, confectionery at Quaker Henry Thorne, military shell-filling at Barnbow and tanks at Vickers – all came on stream to supplement wool.

After 1755 oil lamps lit up the streets. In 1777, next to the White Cloth Hall, the Assembly Rooms for hosting balls and card games was built and in the 1780s the Park Estate around elegant Georgian Park Place took shape with its unique and breathtaking Moorish building – a design forerunner of the splendid mosques which were built in the city in the twentieth century; the merchants in Park Place have now been replaced with modern commercial enterprises. On Hunslet Lane the Theatre Royal opened, followed by music halls in Albion Street and Vicar Lane. Leeds's voluminous library opened in 1768, moving to Commercial Street. Today it remains the oldest surviving subscription library in England. The Blue Coat charity school was built in 1705 and Mary Potter's almshouses were constructed in 1736. Fine Renaissance and ancient architecture was very much in evidence: ecclesiastically, Holy Trinity church was consecrated in the 1720s, modelled on a Roman basilica, while industrial chimneys mirrored Italian campaniles, and an impressive mill building imitated an Egyptian temple, notable for its flat turfed roof where sheep gently grazed – until they made a habit of falling off onto the road below.

In 1801 the population of Leeds was 30,000. By the standards of the time it was now a large town. In 1851, it was home to 101,000 people. The Industrial Revolution fuelled population growth. Leeds' particular industrial resurgence had been galvanised by the opening of the Aire & Calder Navigation in 1699, the Leeds and Liverpool Canal in 1816 giving access to the US market via Liverpool, and the railways from 1834 – the first line was the Leeds and Selby Railway opened on 22 September 1834. The first Leeds railway station was at Marsh Lane; the Leeds Wellington station opened in 1848; the Central in 1854, and the New Station in 1869. Gradually, the town was linking up with major towns and ports throughout the north of England. In many areas Leeds was cutting edge: Leeds Bridge was the setting for the first moving pictures made with a single-lens camera in 1888.

Things really took off for Leeds with the establishment of the mighty cloth mills of the Industrial Revolution and the introduction of machinery, which was the catalyst for mass production. The first mills were the Park Mills of Bean Ing

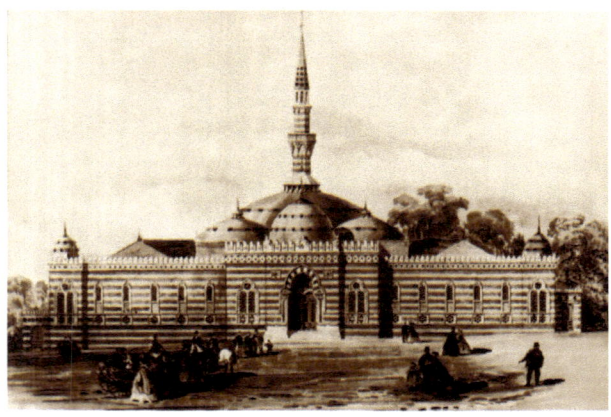

One other distinctly exotic building was the Oriental Baths, opposite the Mechanics' Institute in Cookridge Street, by Cuthbert Broderick – built in 1866, renovated in 1882.

in west Leeds under Benjamin Gott, the owner of a cloth-merchant firm called Wormald, Fountaine & Gott. Bean Ing is where the *Yorkshire Post* building is now.

Between 1790 and 1800, Gott excelled in the production of superfine cloth. Gott's production was greater than anything achieved before – the British and the Swedish Armies were among his many accounts. Armley Mills, established by Gott in 1806, is now Leeds Industrial Museum. Gott got his well-deserved statue which stands in Armley church. John Marshall, that other great industrialist, was nothing if not architecturally flamboyant: his flax mills in Holbeck are still there on Marshall Street but his most famous and splendidly unorthodox is a full-scale replica of the ancient Egyptian temple at Edfu, opened 1838. The Temple of Edfu is dedicated to the falcon god Horus, built some time in the Ptolemaic period between 237 and 57 BC.

Leeds parish church was built in an eighteenth-century Romantic style, and the corn exchange was modelled spectacularly on a Roman coliseum and topped off by a huge elliptical dome reminiscent of Rome's Pantheon. Kirkgate Market, that famous Victorian covered market opened its stalls. Leeds station boasts a spaghetti art deco concourse above the fantastic Dark Arches which straddle the river. If nothing else this extraordinary development proves that Victorian Leeds architects loved a challenge. Many of the mid-nineteenth-century buildings erected in Leeds were designed by Hull architect Cuthbert Broderick. His triumphs include Leeds Town Hall (opened by Queen Victoria in 1858), the Leeds Mechanics' Institute, the Civic Theatre and the domed corn exchange of 1861 mentioned above. The dome was designed to allow sunlight in so that merchants could easily scrutinise and assess the quality of the grain they were buying. Then there is the art gallery with its quintessentially Yorkshire Atkinson Grimshaws, and the breathtaking Victorian arcades, still chic and elegant after all these years, which include the magnificent Thornton's Arcade (1877) and the County Arcade.

In 1893 Leeds became a city officially. The first police force went on the beat in 1836, Beckett Street cemetery was opened in 1845, and Leeds United was founded in 1919. Other industries included many to support the textile industries: machinery for spinning, machine tools, steam engines and gears, chemicals and leather and pottery. Leeds was a steel city too. Coal was mined nearby and the Middleton Railway, the first successful commercial steam locomotive railway in the world, transported that coal into central Leeds for domestic and industrial use. The track was the first rack railway and the locomotive which ran on it, *Salamanca*, was the first to operate on twin cylinders. The city centre became a major transport and commercial centre; Hunslet and Holbeck were by now prominent engineering hubs. Armley, Bramley and Kirkstall built their mills.

This prodigious industrial development obviously drove construction on an extensive scale and saw the building of mills, factories, railway stations and other facilities to support industrial and commercial expansion. These edifices, as we shall see, still characterise and inform the Leeds cityscape and its skylines.

By 1841 the population of Leeds was 88,000. At the end of the century the *Yorkshire Factory Times* described Leeds as 'a vast business place ... a

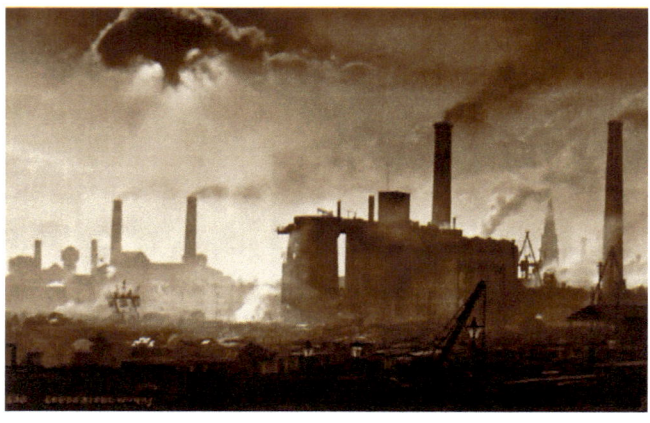

An unfamiliar view of Leeds showing it as a steel city belching smoke. Hunslet parish church is visible in the background. (Photograph taken by Keith Greenhalf)

miniature London'. A latter-day powerhouse of the north? On 11 September 1858 *The Illustrated London News* reported that Leeds was the 'largest and most flourishing' city in Yorkshire, the fifth in England 'in point of population and commercial activity. The population in 1851 was 172,270. The number of inhabited houses that year was 36,165.'

1878 saw the Grand Theatre curtain go up for its premiere. In 1901 the population of Leeds stood at 178,000 and rising. In 1874 the Yorkshire College of Science threw open its doors; Leeds University was founded in 1904 from this very college. St Anne's RC Cathedral was built; Leeds city market opened in 1904. Leeds' first cinema ushered in the silver screen in 1905. In 1925, St James' Hospital was founded and in 1933 Leeds Civic Hall was built. Leeds General Infirmary, originally opened in 1868 as the New Infirmary in Infirmary Street, was expanded in line with rapidly increasing community demand and advances in medical science.

As in other cities, Leeds faced a critical housing problem with many of its squalid back-to-backs condemned as unfit for human habitation. In the interwar years, sprawling council estates and new private housing were built. The most interesting, and one of the most disastrous, of these schemes was Quarry Hill Flats, built between 1935 and 1941, providing a roof for over 3,000 people. In the Second World War seventy-seven Leeds people were killed and 197 buildings were destroyed. Air raid shelters were hastily built. The post-war years were witness to more temporary accommodation in the shape of prefabs (known locally as flat tops or t'piggerys), yet there were now more housing estates, high-rise flats, new schools and public facilities.

As traditional Leeds industries declined, so tourism started to become a significant force in the local economy. Leeds was now a focus for such modern industries as retail and media; call centres and offices proliferated and the skyline changed beyond recognition. Leeds was home for *The Yorkshire Post*, The Yorkshire Bank, Yorkshire Electricity and Yorkshire Television. Montague Burton's bespoke tailoring factory on Hudson Road employed 16,000 people at its peak and was the largest clothing company in Europe.

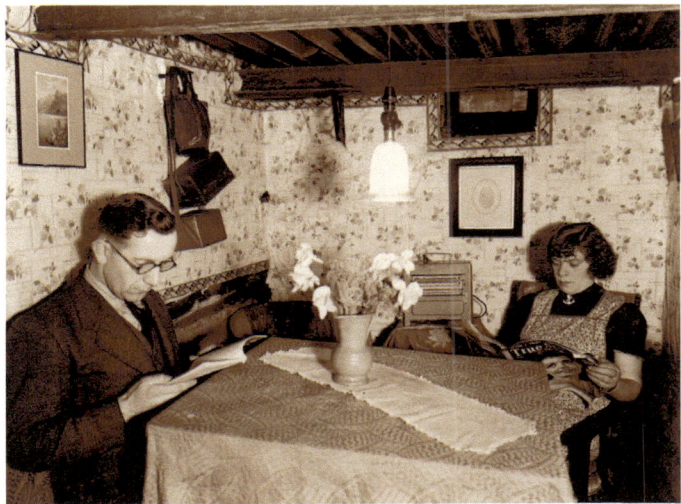

Mr and Mrs Horace Fawcett in their air raid shelter, October 1940, in Cardigan Avenue, Burley – actually a very comfortable reinforced coal cellar. The Leodis website tells that

> The Fawcetts were held up as a shining example of resourcefulness and ingenuity. When members of the ARP came to inspect this shelter, they found the walls neatly papered, electric lighting and a heater installed, chairs and a table, and pictures on the wall, with a cot for the baby in the corner. 'It is a grand piece of work' was the comment of Councillor H. W. Sellars, ARP chairman.

Many others just moaned about their shelters. (Courtesy of Leodis; © Leeds Library & Information Services)

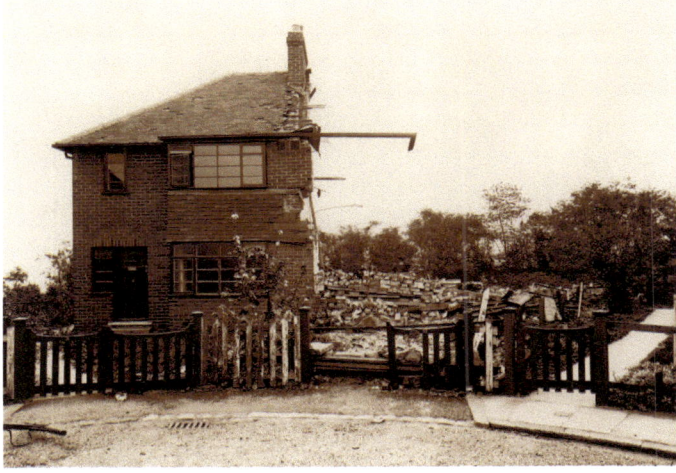

The Luftwaffe converts a semi-detached to a detached house on 22 September 1941. The victim was at No. 11 Cliff Side Gardens, a cul-de-sac off Cliff Road. Apparently, the owners had taken shelter in next door's cellar because they themselves did not have a cellar. (Courtesy of Leodis, © Leeds Library & Information Services)

The curtains went up at Leeds Playhouse in 1970, moving to a new building in 1989. The wonderful Royal Armouries Museum opened in 1995 and the fascinating Thackray Medical Museum followed in 1997. The Henry Moore Institute and Gallery opened in Leeds, quite rightly so as he was a student at the art school here. The Monet Garden in Roundhay Park sprang to life in 1999.

Shopping centres spread like a rash throughout the city: the Merrion Shopping Centre was built in 1964 and in the early 1970s the Bond Street Centre opened its doors, later to be refurbished and rebadged as Leeds Shopping Plaza. St John's Shopping Centre was built in 1983 and White Rose Shopping Centre opened in 1997. Then there was The Light and Trinity in 2013; the arrival of Harvey Nichols led to Leeds being called 'Knightsbridge of the North'. In the early '70s a major development was the pedestrianisation of Leeds city centre.

In the twenty-first century, Leeds functions as one of eight core cities in the Core City Group that act as a hub to their respective regions; it is regarded as the principal city of the ceremonial county of West Yorkshire. Leeds is a vital new media and technology entrepot. Around 35 per cent of the country's email traffic is clicked from here and it is the second largest IT employer in England. Leeds Arena provides a state of the art concert venue to equal anything in the country. £647 million has been spent on new office developments in the city in recent years. Currently, it is celebrated as one of the key urban components in the much-vaunted but as yet unfinanced 'powerhouse of the north'. Only time will tell…

The 50 Buildings

1. The White Cloth Hall (1711), Kirkgate

Leeds, lying on the fringes of the Yorkshire cloth-producing district had to compete for trade with better placed neighbouring towns, so in 1711 all the cloth business was centralised in the purpose-built first White Cloth Hall on Kirkgate from Briggate. Indeed, Leeds' White Cloth Hall was a direct riposte to the merchants of Wakefield, who, in an undisguised attempt to attract business away from Leeds, built a cloth hall to house their market. This was much better than the Leeds market at the time, being indoors and protected from the weather. Leeds merchants had no choice but to do the same, and a cloth hall for the trading of white (that is, undyed) cloth was built on Kirkgate on a site provided by Lord Irwin of Temple Newsam with £1,000 contributed by merchants and tradesmen. Thoresby describes it as 'built upon Pillars and Arches in the form of an Exchange, with a Quadrangular Court within'. The new White Cloth Hall was built on the site of some former almshouses. Some white cloth continued to be sold in Briggate. The White Cloth building is still there.

Predictably, perhaps, the Leeds trade soon outgrew the cloth hall and in 1755 the clothiers financed the building of the second White Cloth Hall south of the river on Meadow Lane. But this second White Cloth Hall also soon proved inadequate, and, smarting at the opening of a rival cloth hall at Gomersal, in 1774 the Leeds merchants agreed on the building of a third hall in Leeds. A site was found on a piece of land called the Tenter Ground in The Calls. The new hall was built around a large central courtyard, and at the northern end it was two storeys high, with assembly rooms on the upper storey. This hall opened in 1775. In 1776 the management of the cloth hall passed from the merchants to the clothiers, and a committee of trustees was set up to be responsible for the organisation of the cloth market.

It was not all hard work and unending business at the Cloth Hall. The central yard was occasionally used for spectacular events, as in 1786 when a Mr Lunardi made a 'balloon ascent from the area of the White Cloth Hall, amid the plaudits of 30,000 people'.

The railways intervened in 1865 when this White Cloth Hall was demolished to make way for the railway; in 1868, as compensation, the railway company built a new hall on King Street. This fourth White Cloth Hall never really got off the ground; it was demolished in 1895. The Met Hotel today occupies the site: the cupola on the hotel roof was once part of the cloth hall.

Not everyone could trade in the cloth halls. Clothiers were obliged to have served a seven-year apprenticeship first, later reduced to five years. Anyone wanting to sell cloth who did not qualify, the so called 'Irregulars', had to use a separate building, which was first in Meadow Lane, and then from 1792 on the ground floor of the Music Hall in Albion Street, known as 'Tom Paine's Hall'.

Not surprisingly, the mixed or coloured cloth-makers, who were still using the open-air market in Briggate, wanted their own cloth hall. Accordingly, a patch of land in the Park was bought – now the site of City Square and Infirmary Street. Each wing of the building was divided into two 'streets' with two rows of stands. It was used by a massive 1,770 clothiers who could buy a stand for £2.10s. The hall, Leeds' largest, cost £5,300 and opened in 1756. The central courtyard could hold 20,000 people. This was also used for public meetings where the steps acted as a platform for the speakers: in 1880 Gladstone addressed a Liberal Party meeting there. A small octagonal building, the Exchange or Rotunda, was later added, used as an office by the trustees who were responsible for the running of the property. The hall was knocked down in 1890, and replaced by the post office in City Square.

The White and Mixed Cloth Halls were highly prestigious institutions and any important visitor to the city was given a guided tour to see the textile markets in operation. One such visitor in 1768 to the Mixed Cloth Hall was the King of Denmark.

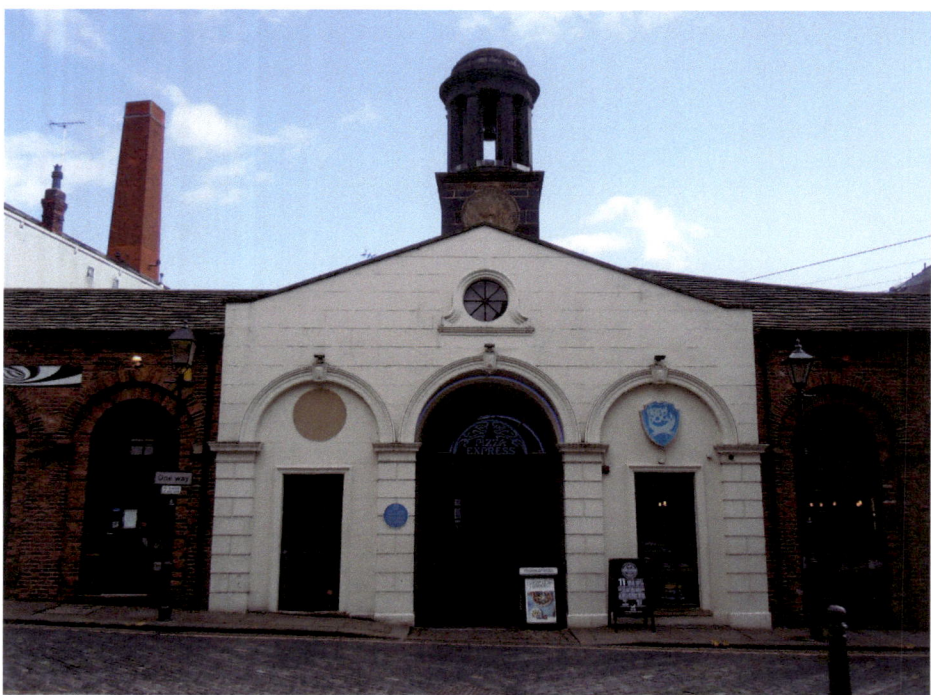

The first White Cloth Hall today, refurbished as a Pizza Express.

2. Whitelocks Ale House (1715), Turk's Head Yard, off Briggate

Grade II-listed, Whitelock's Ale House first opened its doors in 1715 as the Turk's Head in, fittingly enough, Turk's Head Yard. The pub was ideally placed to cater for the traders and customers thronging Briggate market. It is Leeds' oldest surviving pub.

In 1867 John Lupton Whitelock, a flautist with the Hallé and Leeds Symphony Orchestra, was granted the licence of the Turk's Head. The Whitelock family bought the pub in the 1880s and in 1886 completed a refurbishment which has left us with the elaborate décor we can still see and enjoy today, including the long marble-topped bar, etched mirrors and glass.

In the mid-1890s the pub was rebadged as Whitelock's First City Luncheon Bar and in 1897 John Lupton Whitelock installed electricity, including an exciting new revolving searchlight, at the Briggate entrance to the yard. Trick beer glasses in which a sovereign was placed ensured the punter got, not the money, but an electric shock.

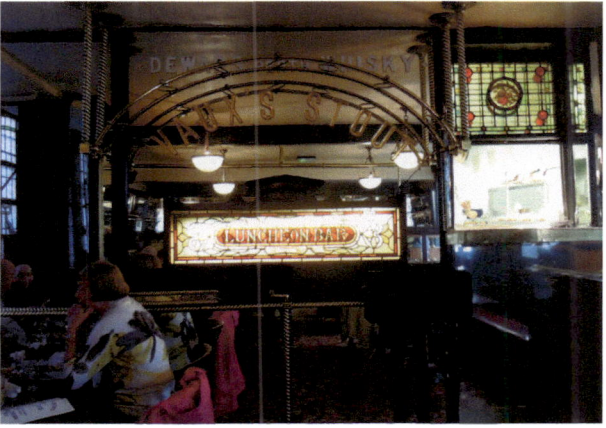

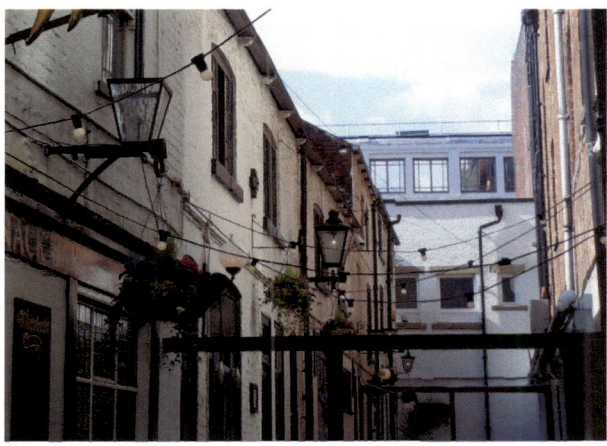

Inside and outside the wonderful Whitelocks.

Prince George (1902–42), later Duke of Kent, threw a party there in a curtained-off section of the restaurant. In those days a doorman ensured that men wore dinner jackets; women were not allowed at the bar, so waiters served drinks to the women where they sat.

John Betjeman described Whitelocks as 'the Leeds equivalent of Fleet Street's Old Cheshire Cheese and far less self-conscious, and does a roaring trade. It is the very heart of Leeds.' It features in *Great Bars of the World* rubbing shoulders with the Long Bar in Shanghai's Peace Hotel and Harry's in Venice.

3. Leeds General Infirmary (1767), Great George Street

The General Infirmary at Leeds (its old official name) goes back to June 1767 when an infirmary 'for the relief of the sick and hurt poor within this parish' was set up in a private house in Kirkgate. Four years later the General Infirmary's first purpose-built building opened near City Square in Infirmary Street on the site of the former Yorkshire Bank; the five founding physicians were all graduates of the University of Edinburgh Medical School. LGI has continued to expand ever since, resulting initially in the move to an impressive new site on Great George Street in 1869. The infirmary buildings here were designed by Sir George Gilbert Scott.

The design of the new hospital was not taken lightly: the Infirmary's chief physician, Dr Charles Chadwick, toured many of the modern hospitals of Europe. He returned favouring the pavilion plan recommended by many doctors and nurses including Florence Nightingale; this then was the plan adopted for the new infirmary, featuring state of the art equipment with lots of baths and toilets and hydraulic hoists to reduce the strenuous physical work required of nurses.

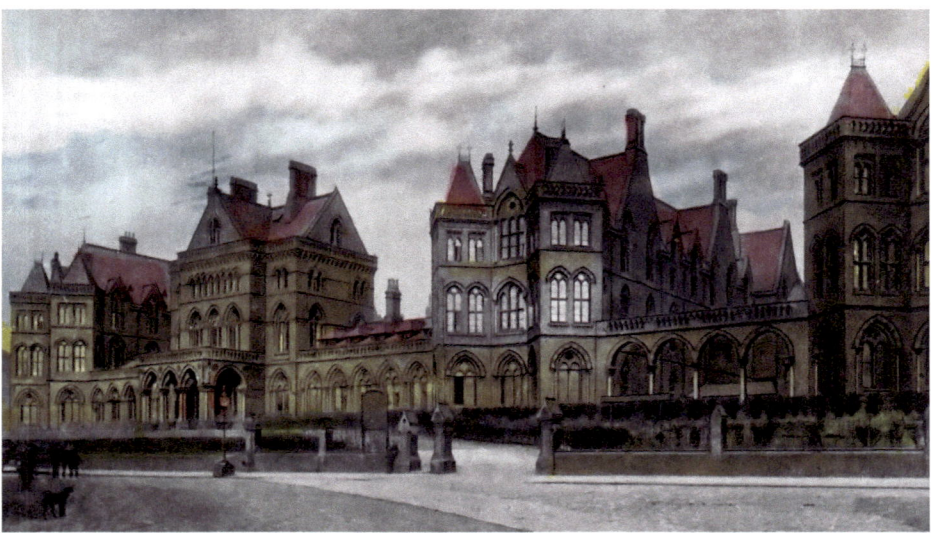

The LGI in 1921.

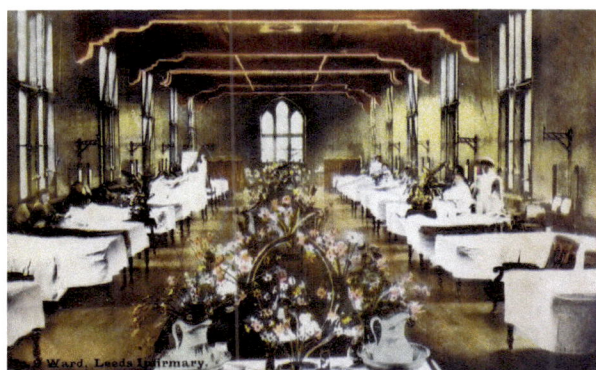

Ward 9 in the LGI in 1908. The card was franked at 9.30 p.m. on the 8 May, sent by Emma to her cousin to warn her that she was coming to visit.

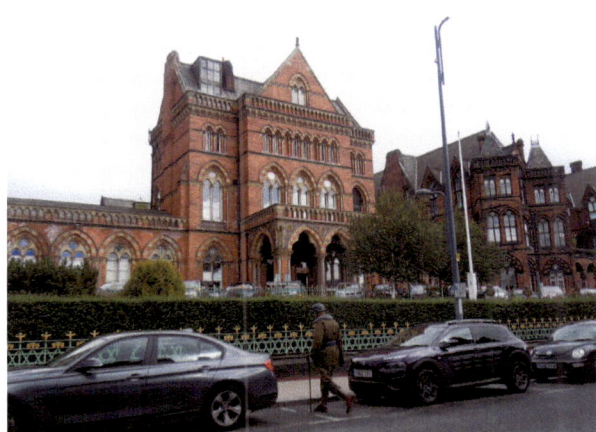

The LGI in 2015 – note the Russian soldier.

4. Armley Mills (1788), Canal Road

Armley Mills and its history reflects the history of the textile industry in Leeds. That long history begins in the mid-sixteenth century when local clothier Richard Booth leased 'Armley Millnes' from Henry Saville. We hear from a 1707 document about 'That fulling mill in Armley ... containing two wheels and four stocks ... also the water corn mill and all the fulling mills ... containing one wheel and two stocks'. By 1788, Armley could boast five waterwheels powering eighteen fulling stocks.

Fulling is one of the end processes in cloth production. It involves pounding the cloth with big hammers in pits filled with water, urine and 'fullers earth', making the fibres mat together or 'felt'. You can still see fulling hammers in the mill today. Urine – a source of ammonia – was collected from nearby families, who saved it up especially for that purpose.

In 1788, Armley Mills was bought by Col Thomas Lloyd, a wealthy Leeds cloth merchant, who made it the world's largest woollen mill. In 1804 Benjamin Gott bought the mills. In November 1805 disaster struck when the mill was almost entirely gutted by fire. Gott rebuilt the mill from fireproof materials, using brick

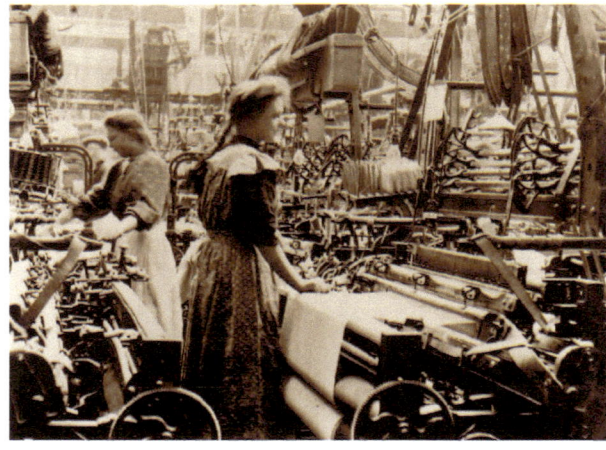

Armley Mills in action around 1900.

and iron wherever possible. The early mills were considerable fire hazards with airborne fibres igniting and setting fire to flammable structures. The 1788 mill had been powered by five waterwheels while the 1805 mill was engined by two metal wheels that went by the names of Wellington and Blucher, allied heroes in the Napoleonic Wars. They were rated at 70 horse power. It is Gott's Mill which you can see today.

Armley Mills went from strength to strength with export markets in North and South America, Europe and the Far East. In 1805 the mill was the world's largest woollen mill, containing eighteen fulling stocks and fifty looms. Gott was one of Britain's largest employers in Britain. After his death in 1840 his sons John and William introduced the first steam engine to Armley Mills in 1850 to supplement the waterwheels which continued operating into the 1860s.

In 1971 the mill closed and was bought by Leeds City Council, reopening in 1982 as Leeds Industrial Museum. Botany Bay Yard is close by – so named because it was the first place in England where wool from Botany Bay in Australia was landed. The museum has collections of textile machinery, railway equipment and heavy engineering.

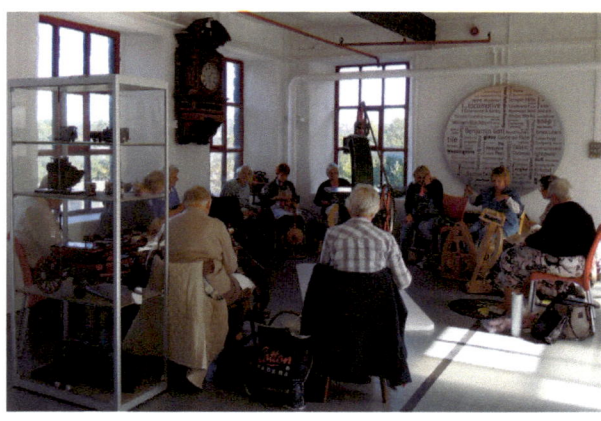

A spinning and weaving group in action in 2015 using replica machinery, Leeds Industrial Museum at Armley Mills.

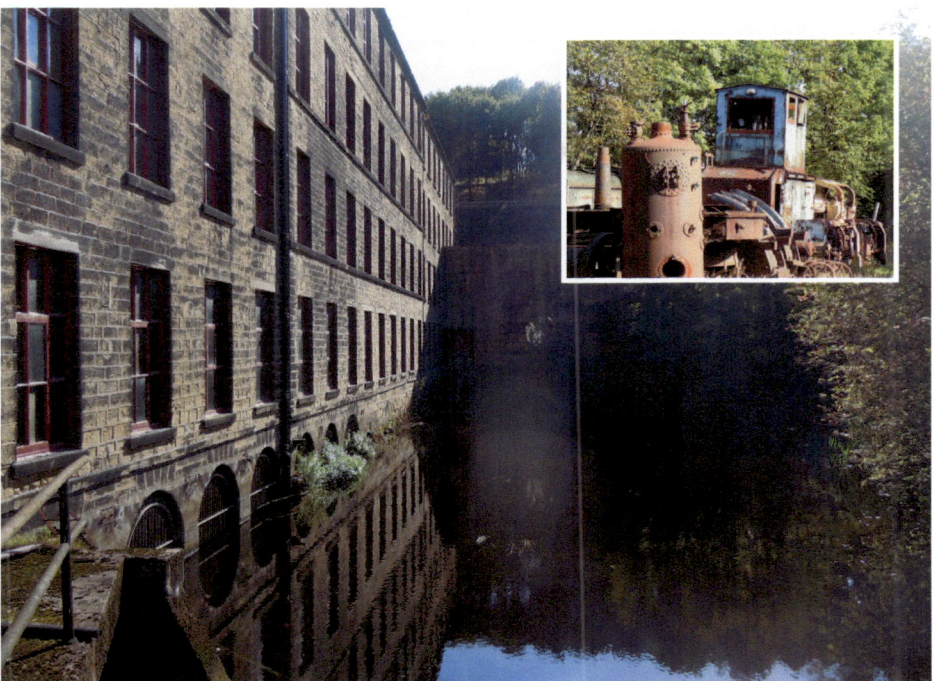

A reflective Armley Mills, October 2015 and (*inset*) one of the rusting hulks awaiting restoration.

5. Marshall's Mill (1792), Marshall Street, Holbeck Urban Village

Holbeck Urban Village is an area in Leeds given over to various urban renewal schemes comprising largely light industrial companies working from renovated mills and former locomotive engineering and buildings. They include Midland Mills, Marshall's Mill, Temple Works, Tower Works and the Round Foundry. There are thirty-three listed buildings in the Holbeck Urban Village conservation boundary, including one Grade I-listed building, and two Grade II-listed buildings.

Marshall's Mill was a flax mill which began working in 1791/92 under industrial pioneer John Marshall – it was a four-storey mill, drawing water from the nearby Hol Beck. It boasted a Boulton & Watt steam engine and was a major catalyst in replacing Yorkshire's hitherto cottage industry of hand-driven spindles. In the nineteenth century more mills, warehouses, engine houses, and reservoirs were added on the south side of Hol Beck. The six-storey Mill 'C' was completed in 1816.

The impressive Temple Mill, designed to replicate an Egyptian temple, as we have seen, was built between 1838 and 1841. Temple Works once contained 'the largest room in the world'. The roof of the building was large enough to have grass planted on its surface, allowing sheep to graze up there.

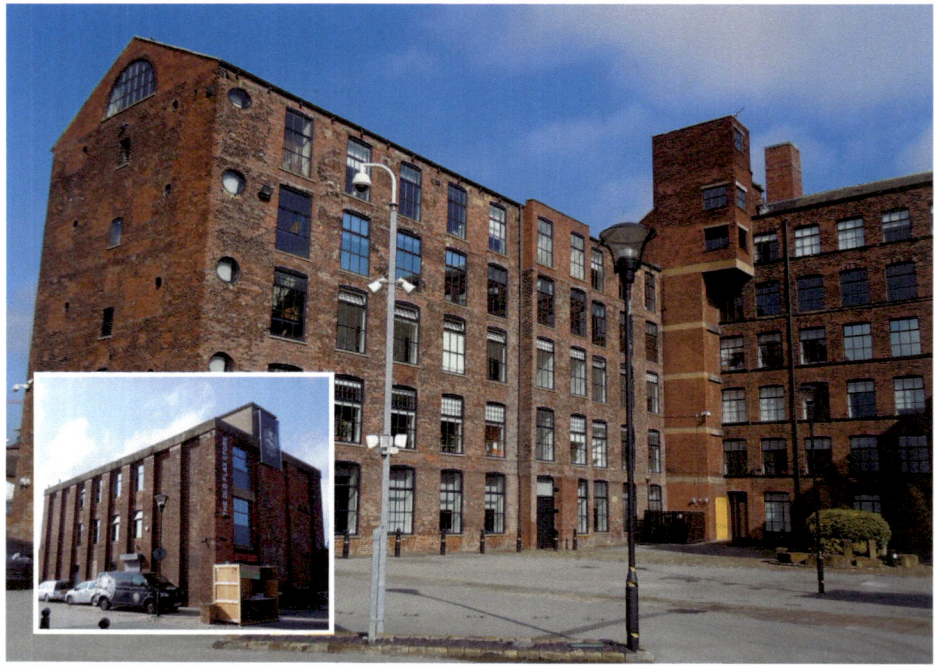

Marshall's Mill and (*inset*) its flax store. Both brilliantly restored and put to good use again. The Round Foundry.

In time, the complex employed over 2,000 factory workers and was one of the largest factories in the world, with 7,000 steam-powered spindles. The addition of the Temple Mill completed the construction of mills by Marshall & Sons on this site. All of the mill buildings added from 1815 still exist.

Child labour was rife: in 1832 it was alleged that 'In Mr Marshall's mill, a boy of nine years of age was stripped to the skin, bound to an iron pillar, and mercilessly beaten with straps, until he fainted.' However, others assert that Marshall treated his workers better than most. Overseers were forbidden to use corporal punishment and Marshall installed fans in an attempt to regulate the temperature in the mill. The end for Marshall & Sons came in 1886 when their site was taken over by other textile manufacturers.

6. The Round Foundry (1797), Water Lane, Holbeck Urban Village

The Round Foundry was built between 1795 and 1797 by Fenton, Murray & Wood. It was here that Matthew Murray cut his teeth as a celebrated engineer, turning out textile machinery, steam engines and the first locomotives for the

Middleton Railway, including *Salamanca*. The Round Foundry was soon to become one of the world's first specialist engineering foundries with substantial global exports.

Fire destroyed some of the original buildings in the nineteenth century, including the unique rotunda that gave the Round Foundry its name; the rotunda allowed more efficient access for machinery. Nevertheless, seven listed buildings survive in the Round Foundry complex including the Dry Sand Foundry, the Green Sand Foundry and No. 101 Water Lane.

The local pub, now called The Cross Keys, was the scene of some intense industrial espionage when Matthew Murray's competitors Boulton and Watt used it as a base to spy on developments at the cutting-edge foundry. The Round Foundry was the first place in Leeds to be lit by gas: Murray lobbied tirelessly for the corporation to follow his example and light its streets in the interests of public safety. Murray made his home on land next to the foundry and ran steam from there to his house, which became known as Steam Hall. It was England's first centrally heated house.

Today, the completion of the first phase of a £30 million redevelopment has seen the genesis of the multi-award-winning Round Foundry Media Centre, which provides office space for creative and digital media companies, restaurants, bars and cafés in a number of courtyards which retain as much of the character of the old foundry as is possible. Stage II opened in 2008 with the first Leeds Brewery pub, Midnight Bell, located here alongside Welcome to Yorkshire, the region's tourism agency among its occupants.

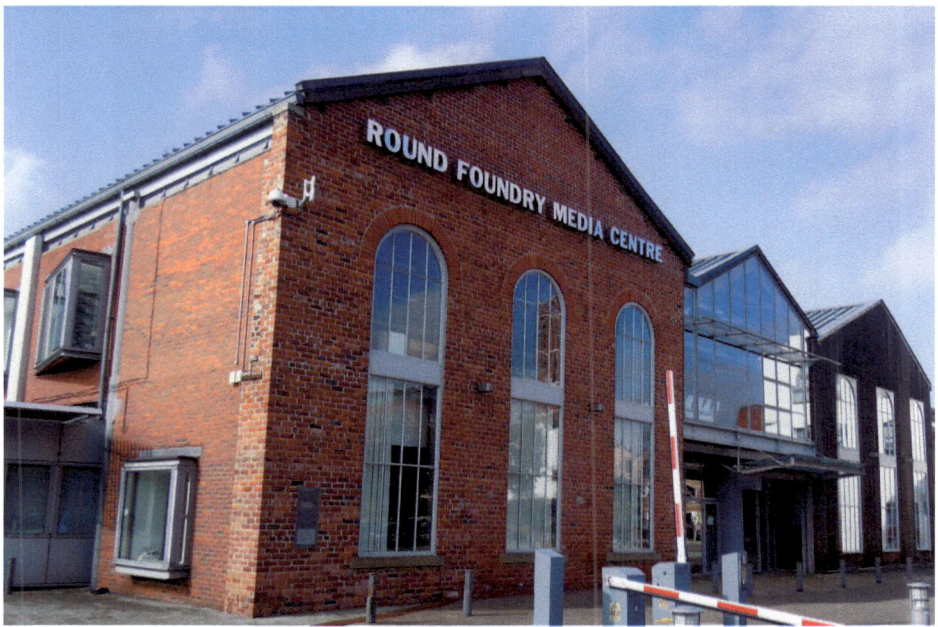

The General Post Office in City Square, in 1915 on a card going to France during the First

7. Midland Mills (1812), Silver Street, Holbeck Urban Village

An enterprising man called John Jubb built the first mill on the site in 1793 but sold his interest in the early nineteenth century to an even more enterprising man, who capitalised on the expansion of the flax spinning industry by diversifying into the manufacture of textile machinery which he sold to local and national mills. He later moved to Meadow Lane and sold the Midland Mills site to the Drabble Brothers, who carried on the manufacture of textile machinery and also patented designs for cart axles. Unfortunately, a disagreement between the two brothers led to bankruptcy in 1812.

Taylor and Wordsworth, two employees of the Drabble brothers, bought the site in 1812 and established Taylor, Wordsworth and Co.; the inventive Wordsworth procured patents for improvements to machinery for spinning, and for heckling and dressing flax. The firm employed around 100 householders, described as the 'highest class of mechanics'. They also made machines to the designs of other inventors.

Curiously, Taylor and Wordsworth both married Drabble girls – Wordsworth married a Martha Drabble in Tankersley, near Barnsley, in 1803 while Taylor married a Hannah Drabble in Leeds in 1805; then, following the death of the first Martha in 1810, Wordsworth married another Martha Drabble in Leeds in 1811.

In 1844 the company organised a firm's excursion to Liverpool with employees of Marshall's Mill – an important customer of theirs. It was something of a daring and groundbreaking event at the time, an event which gave even the editor of the normally liberal *Leeds Mercury* some cause for concern:

> Entirely approving of excursions for the working class, and with the kindest feelings towards the workmen of Messrs Marshall and Messrs Taylor and Wordsworth, we would express our earnest hope that the Sunday spent in Liverpool may not in any respect be spent in a manner unbecoming the day, and that every prudential care will be exercised to keep the younger hands under the guardianship of the more experienced, so that no moral harm may result from an excursion calculated otherwise to be so agreeable and improving. There are many excellent men among the above bodies of workmen, and great responsibility will rest upon them for the issue of this new and somewhat doubtful experiment, of a large body of people being away from home on the Sabbath, and on two whole nights.

By 1888, the works extended over an area exceeding 3 acres. In an account which confirms the firm's position at the centre of the Leeds textile industry it is recorded that,

> … The premises consist of a number of substantial buildings, mostly four storeys in height, and regularly grouped according to the branch of the machine-making department to which such building is allotted. The firm makes every description of machinery that is used in the woollen, silk, and flax manufacturing, and in the dyeing and finishing trades, and they have been awarded several gold medals where their machines have been exhibited for the superiority and finish of the machinery.

In the 1930s Platts bought the factory – soon to become the world's largest textile machine-makers, employing over 15,000 people. The factory ceased trading in 1981, effectively marking the end of the textile industry in Leeds.

8. The Old Post Office (1813), City Square

What was to become the old post office building was originally built as a courthouse in 1813 until the judiciary decamped to the new town hall in 1858. The post office moved into the building in 1864 adding a further storey in 1872 for the postal telegraph. It was all demolished in 1897 after a new post office had been built between Infirmary Street and Quebec Street. Old photographs show the telegraph receiver on the roof. The post office was converted in 2006 to luxury holiday apartments.

The Square was officially opened on 16 September 1903. Apart from the Old post office there was the original Queen's Hotel on Wellington Street, which

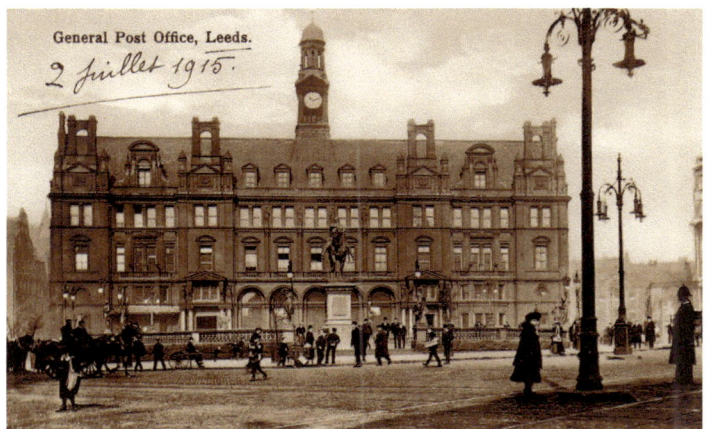

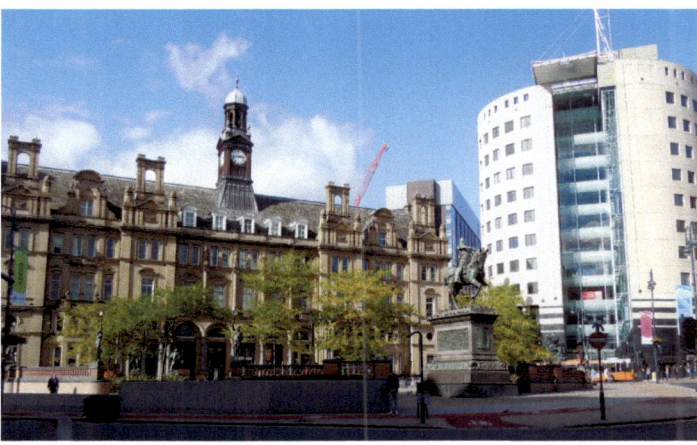

World War; and a century later in 2015 with No. 1 City Square office building on the right. The Standard Life Assurance Building was the first building to stand there, built in 1901. It was demolished and rebuilt by Norwich Union in 1967, then demolished again in 1995 to be replaced by No. 1 City Square.

opened in 1863 and was later demolished to make way for the present Queen's Hotel, built in 1936. The 186-room Park Plaza Hotel on the corner of Boar Lane and Park Row occupies Royal Exchange House. Today the impressive building at No. 1 City Square is on the site of the 1901 Standard Life Assurance building, which was replaced by the Norwich Union building in 1967. This was demolished in 1995. Down Infirmary Street leading off from the square, the post office building is on the left and then there is the former Yorkshire Penny Bank building with its distinctive tower. This is on the site of the first infirmary from 1771, which was opened by the Duke of Devonshire on 17 August 1894 with a golden key.

Some fine statues embellish City Square, the grandest of which is a bronze Black Prince on horseback. There are also statues of local heroes: Joseph Priestley, founding father of modern chemistry; John Harrison, early woollen cloth merchant and Leeds benefactor; James Watt of steam engine fame; and Dr Walter Farquhar Hook, the vicar behind the establishment of twenty-one churches in Leeds, as well as of eight nymphs and some elegant light standards. The Black Prince (son of Edward III) has nothing to do with Leeds; he was a gift from Col Thomas Walter Harding, Lord Mayor of Leeds between 1898 and 1899 and was just someone Harding admired, symbolising as he did democracy and chivalry.

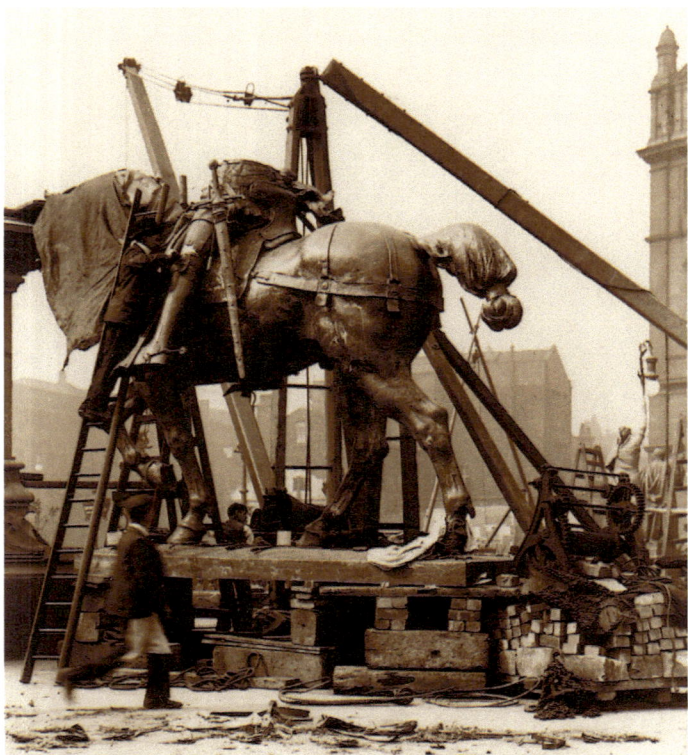

The Black Prince getting himself together in City Square. It took seven years to complete and was cast in Belgium because it was too big for any British foundry. The Black Prince was brought to City Square by barge from Hull along the Aire and Calder Navigation and unveiled on 16 September 1903. (Courtesy of Leodis; © Leeds Library & Information Services)

9. Leeds City Museum (1819), Park Row

The museum began life in 1819, established on Park Row by the Leeds Philosophical and Literary Society, and opened to the public in 1821. In 1941, the museum building and many displays and artefacts were badly damaged by bombing. The museum closed in 1965 but reopened in 2008 in the refurbished Mechanics' Institute Building. One of the most popular exhibits is the infamous Leeds Tiger. It was saved from the curators' skip by the *Yorkshire Post* when it mounted a successful campaign to retain it as a popular centrepiece of the museum's collection.

The Leeds Tiger was originally a tiger-skin rug when presented to the museum in the nineteenth century; the tiger had been shot for taking an unhealthy interest in a village in India. The pelt was then sewn with other tiger skins, and instead of being mounted properly it was stuffed rather amateurishly with straw. The reputation of and affection for the tiger meanwhile escalated. From being just a curious observer of Indian village life, it was elevated to the legendary status of a serial killer of forty villagers.

Another highlight is the Ancient Worlds gallery, which includes a striking Roman floor mosaic from 250 CE around discovered at Aldborough. It depicts the she-wolf (lupa) which suckled Romulus and Remus, legendary founders of Rome in 753 BCE. There are Hellenistic Greek tomb doors from around 250 BCE carved in marble, in bas relief, and the 3,000-year-old Leeds Mummy, Nesyamun, which survived the 1941 bombing raids (two other mummies were destroyed), and is displayed with a reconstruction of his face. Finally, it has an iron replica of a Hellenistic Greek head of Aphrodite – the original was discovered in 1872 at Satala (now Sadak) in north-eastern Turkey and is now in the British Museum.

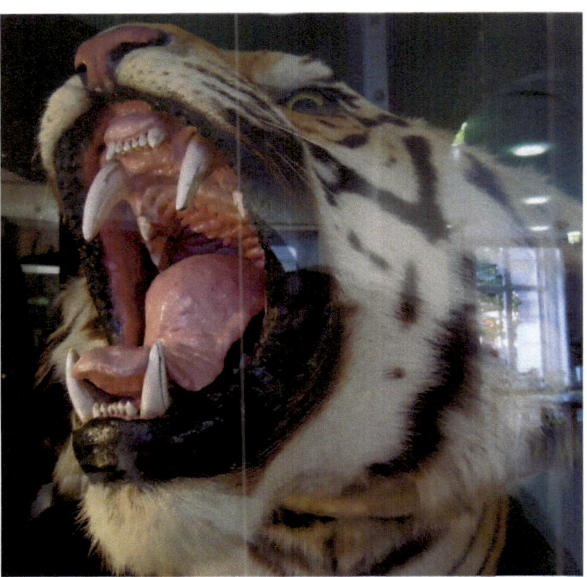

The Leeds Tiger today – roughly stuffed, angry and hungry.

Leeds Mechanics' Institute (1824) was built by Cuthbert Broderick. The objective of the mechanics' institutes was to furnish a technical education for the working man and for professionals to 'address societal needs by incorporating fundamental scientific thinking and research into engineering solutions'. They effectively transformed science and technology education for the man in the street. A number of them have become cutting-edge universities. The world's first opened in Edinburgh in 1821 as the School of Arts of Edinburgh, later Heriot-Watt University. This was followed in 1823 by the Institute in Glasgow, which was founded on the site of the institution set up in 1800 by George Birkbeck and the Andersonian University offering free lectures on arts, science and technical subjects; it moved to London in 1804, became The London Mechanics' Institute from 1823 and, later, Birkbeck College. Liverpool opened in July 1823 and Manchester (later to become UMIST) in 1824. By 1850, there were over 700 Mechanics' Institutes in the UK and abroad, many of which developed into libraries, colleges and universities. Mechanics' institutes provided free lending libraries and also offered lectures, laboratories, and occasionally, as with Glasgow, a museum.

Leeds is a case in point. In 1846, the Leeds Mechanics' Institute was already offering drawing classes when it merged with the Literary Institute, creating Leeds School of Art. In 1868 Leeds Mechanics' Institute becomes the Leeds Institute of Science, Art, and Literature. In 1903, it moved to the Vernon Street building, whose radical design reflected the art & craft movement. Henry Moore and Barbara Hepworth are among the alumni, enrolling in 1919 and 1920, respectively. By 1946, fifteen past students had subsequently been appointed as principals of schools of art. Over time, new design departments were established, including furniture, graphic design and printmaking. A new pottery and workshops were built, and in 1959 a new library was opened. In the mid-1980s the Blenheim Walk building was built.

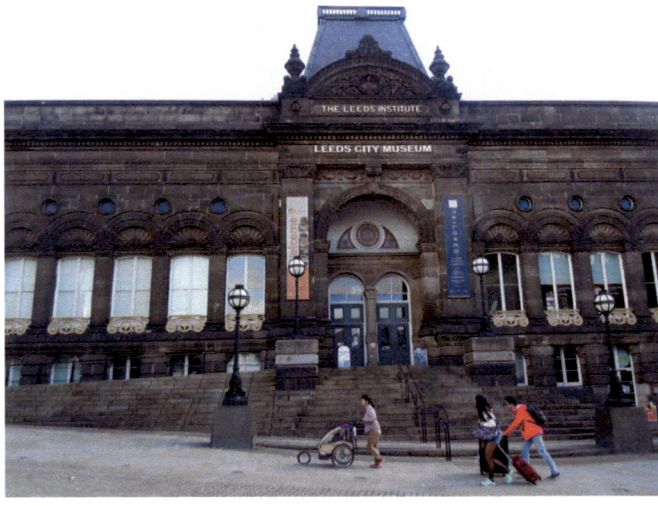

The Mechanics' Institute today, now Leeds City Museum.

Today the Mechanics' Institute, as we have seen, hosts Leeds City Museum – resplendent with its marvellous interior. The circular central hall, originally a lecture room with balcony and ionic columns, has its floor raised on cast-iron columns. This, 'the Albert Hall', was designed to accommodate up to 1,500 people, and was lit by clerestory windows. Around the perimeter were a library, reading room, workshops and studios, classrooms (including one set aside for moral instruction), and dining rooms.

When the Mechanics' Institute stopped educating, it became a concert hall, known as the Civic Theatre, and later, the City Museum.

10. Time Ball Buildings, Nos 24–26 Briggate (c. 1820)

A precious and rare surviving example of elaborate and ornate Victorian-Edwardian shop innovation and design. The premises had a number of occupants over the years: distiller, saddler and trunk-maker, a barber and perfumer and a stationer through the nineteenth century until 1871 when Boar Lane was being rebuilt and the premises were empty. In 1872 J. Dyson, watchmaker, was at No. 26 and by 1872 occupied the whole building.

Most of the elaborate façade was added by Dyson. Bay windows flank the large pedimented clock case at No. 25 and No. 26. At No. 24, Father Time surmounts a large framed clock on the third storey. There are ironwork spandrels, the letters D. & S., and the words 'Tempus Fugit'. Gold lettering shows the date as 1865. The stunning gilded time ball mechanism was linked to Greenwich and dropped at precisely 1.00 p.m. each day; this feature, together with the window mechanism, which raised and lowered the window displays, allowing safe storage in the vaults each night, makes Dyson's unique.

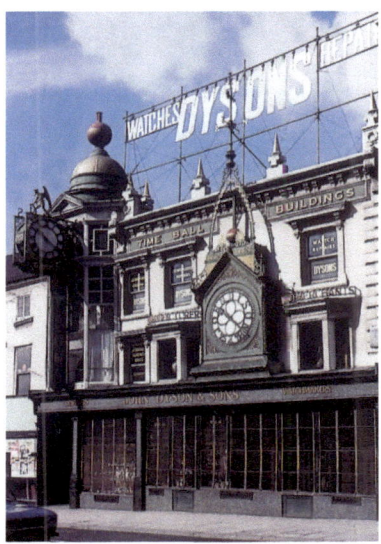

Time Ball Buildings with spectacular advertising.

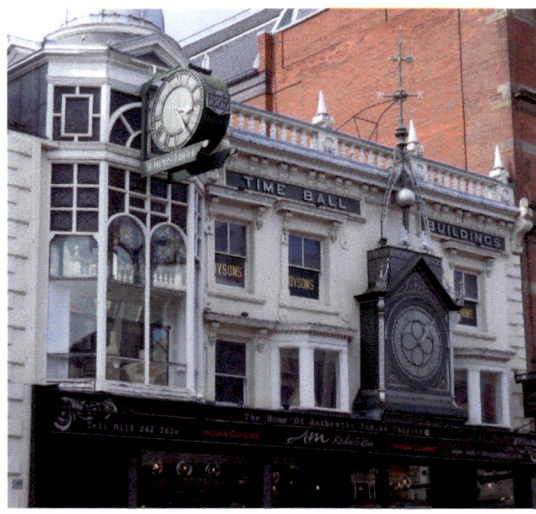

The wonderful building, now with ubiquitous Indian restaurant below.

11. Kirkstall Brewery (1833), Broad Lane, Kirkstall

Kirkstall Brewery is synonymous in some ways with twelfth-century Cistercian Kirkstall Abbey. Indeed, Yorkshire's first pub was the alehouse in which Samuel Ellis started brewing in 953 at Bardsey, to the north of Leeds. It is still there under the guise once of the Priest's Inn and then of the Bingley Arms, but it is significant to us because of the Kirkstall Abbey monks who drank there on the way to St Mary's Abbey in York. Not only did they refresh themselves on their journeys but they brewed ale at the abbey itself – you might call this the first Kirkstall Brewery.

Our Kirkstall Brewery operated between 1833 and 1983 when it was closed by Whitbread. The brewery buildings have been well preserved and now provide accommodation for 1,000 or so Leeds Metropolitan University students at what is now Kirkstall Brewery Student Village. This project was undertaken by the then Leeds Metropolitan, now Beckett University. A new Kirkstall Brewery has been established nearby with many echoes of the original: the old brewery crest, product names, and even their flagship 6 per cent beer, Dissolution Extra IPA, brewed from an original export beer from the 1860s.

The original buildings are Grade II listed, built on either side of the Leeds and Liverpool Canal. You can still see on one of the buildings on the west side of the canal, The Warehouse, the doors just above the water level that were used to load beer barrels onto barges. By 1898 the brewery was producing around 72,000 barrels of beer a year, sold locally and as far away as Australia and New Zealand. Dutton's Blackburn Brewery Ltd purchased Kirkstall Brewery Co. Ltd and its subsidiaries, Albion Brewery (Leeds) Ltd and Willow Brewery Co. Ltd, in 1936 and later renamed it as Dutton's Lancashire & Yorkshire Brewery Corporation Ltd. Duttons was bought by Whitbread in 1957; Kirkstall Brewery was refurbished while the production of bitter and mild went up to quarter of a million barrels a year.

A fascinating revelation was made during renovation of the buildings when it was discovered that a Second World War submarine engine was installed at the brewery as power back-up. This engine was one of a pair built in 1943 but was never actually installed in a submarine. The size of a Ford Transit van, it was sold in 1948 to the brewery and now resides at the Anson Engine Museum in Poynton, Cheshire, being restored.

12. The Hunslet Mill and Victoria Works Complex (1838), Goodman Street

Hunslet Mill was providing work for some 1,500 women engaged in reeling flax for a firm of linen manufacturers called Richard Buckton & Son from 1868 and then by blanket weavers Dodgson & Hargreaves from the mid-1920s until its closure in 1966. It was the largest single-build mill in Leeds.

Victoria Works was completed in 1838. It was occupied by a company of tailors called Botterill & Senior from the 1930s and later was owned by a firm of ironmongers called R. H. Bruce before they vacated in the early 1970s.

Both are Grade II listed and were designed by William Fairbairn, the leading engineer and designer of mill buildings in the first half of the nineteenth century; he can count Armley Mills and Saltaire Mill in his portfolio. Hunslet Mill is a seven-storey red-brick building; the offices retain some fine Greek/Egyptian-style plasterwork on the ceilings. As we know, fire was an ever-present hazard in mills so the entire construction was built to resist fire, with cast-iron columns and inverted T-section beams supporting brick-arched floors.

In 2001 permission was granted to convert the building into 700 flats with amenities and a café but the plans went nowhere. The buildings are in a parlous, dilapidated state and are crying out for sympathetic redevelopment.

13. The Electric Press (1840), Millenium Square

The Electric Press building was built around 1840 and now houses a wide range of upmarket restaurants. It is also home to the Carriageworks Theatre, Leeds City Council's theatre, and Leeds Beckett University's Faculty of Arts, Environment and Technology.

The Grade II-listed Stansfield Chambers were originally the home of the West Riding Carriage Manufactory. The chambers were built in 1848 for this purpose and now gives its name to the theatre Portland Chambers, which was built at the end of the nineteenth century. The buildings were occupied by a variety of tenants over the years up until 1999, including Chorley and Pickersgill printing works. Chorley and Pickersgill are world renowned for printing many of the iconic LNER travel posters from the 1920s onwards.

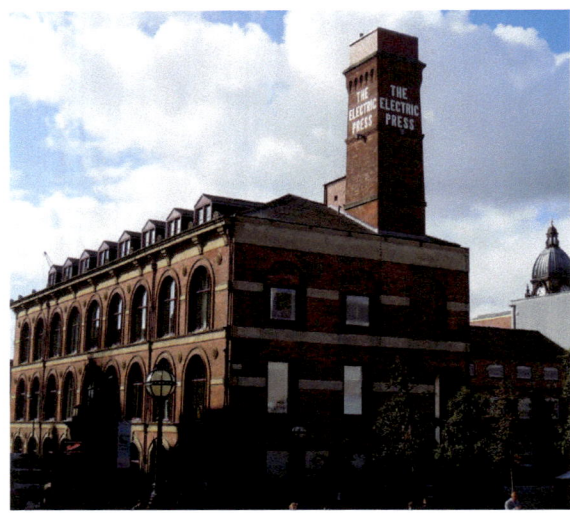

The Electric Press today, converted to house Revolution bar.

The city's first known printer was John Hirst who began printing the *Leeds Mercury* in 1718. By 1810, Leeds still had only eight printing houses but by 1820 things changed dramatically as the numbers mushroomed. By 1911, printing was the fourth largest employer in the city, employing up to 8,000 people. Prominent Leeds printers included Alfred Cooke's, established in 1866; in 1895 they had built what was the world's largest printworks on Hunslet Road. Another was John Waddington Ltd, a company which started off printing theatre posters around 1900 but then shrewdly diversified into games and packaging – Monopoly is their most famous game taking its first roll of the dice in 1935. By 1993, Waddingtons employed 2,700 people in Leeds.

14. Temple Works (1840), Marshall Street, Holbeck Urban Village

A Grade I-listed Victorian former flax mill that has gone down in history as containing the largest room in the world, with sheep grazing on a skylit roof amid an industrially revolutionised Leeds. The breathtaking façade is modelled on the Temple of Horus at Edfu in Egypt. Temple Works was designed by Joseph Bonomi the Younger and constructed by John Marshall between 1836 and 1840.

To this day it is referred to in schools of architecture and engineering the world over not just for the truly awesome façade but also for the unique and visionary engineering solution used for the main mill floor, reminiscent of Frank Lloyd Wright's Johnson Wax Building completed one hundred years later in Racine, Wisconsin. Up until 1981 it was the northern headquarters of the mail-order catalogue company Kay's from 1953 until its closure in 1981 when they moved to a four-storey warehouse in Sweet Street. Kay's was the largest employer in south Leeds.

From 2009 Temple Works Leeds has been a thriving cultural hub that is given over to 20 per cent heritage and education, 40 per cent location shoots and in-house studio events, and 40 per cent public events.

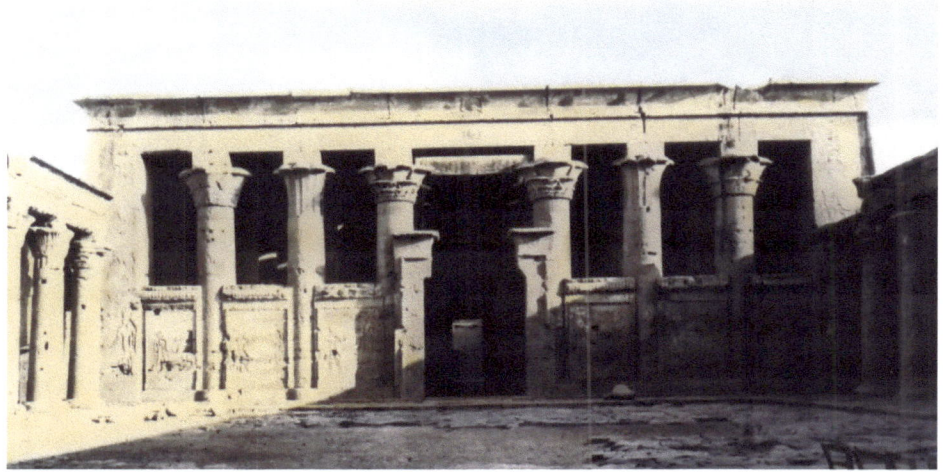

The original Temple of Horus at Edfu as John Marshall might have seen it.

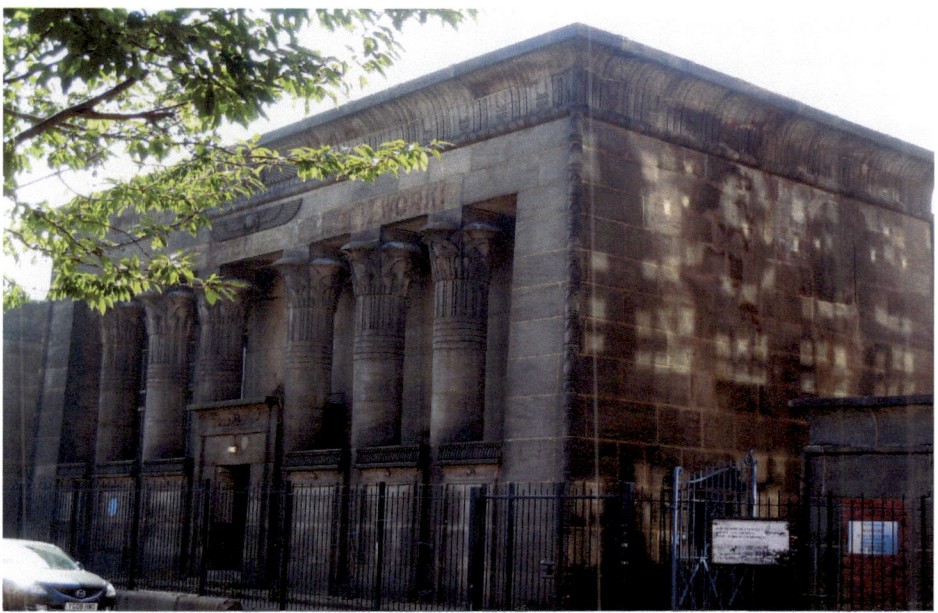

Joseph Bonomi the Younger's Leeds temple – no sign of any sheep today. Apart from this wonderful façade, Bonomi was also responsible for *Nineveh and its Palaces* and other works on Egypt, Nubia, and Ethiopia, illustrated with his own drawings; a house, The Camels, at Wimbledon; and for inventing a machine for measuring the proportions of the human body, about which *The Proportion of the Human Figure* was published in 1856.

Temple Works, or Temple Mill, comprised an office block and factory, the former being based on the temple at Antaeopolis and Temple of Horus at Edfu with a chimney in the shape of an obelisk; the factory building was modelled on the Typhonium at Dendera. Benjamin Hick's 240-HP beam engine featured Egyptian details including a regulator in the form of a winged solar disk. The Egyptian influence came from Marshall's intense interest in Egyptology. The sheep were not just a gimmick: they helped retain humidity in the flax mill to prevent the linen thread from becoming dried out and unworkable. Sheep, of course, are not very good at climbing ladders or stairs so, to get them onto the roof and down again, the hydraulic lift had to be invented – and so it was.

According to Susan Williamson, director of the cultural project Temple Works Leeds,

The roof was originally grassed and mowed by sheep. It was grassed to wick the moisture from the air and bring it down the rainwater pipes to make steam with water from the nearby Hold Beck to power all of the machinery here. With all of the solar energy gained from the skylights, it was able to have a solid 78-degree temperature to keep the air moist and keep the flax from breaking.

In 1842 there was trouble at the mill with the Plug Plot Riots (the 1842 General Strike). They acquired the name 'Plug' because the mills 'were stopped from working by the removal or "drawing" of a few bolts or "plugs" in the boilers so as to prevent steam from being raised' (OED).

The Leeds Annals described the events:

The vicinity of the new mill in Marshall Street was completely crammed with an excited mob, many of whom were armed with bludgeons, stones & c. The yard-door leading to the boilers of the new mill was strongly defended by Mr J. G. Marshall, and a number of workmen; but the mob by repeated efforts forced down the door, and rushed into the yard. They could not find the plug of the boiler, and consequently did not succeed in stopping the mill. They left the premises without having done any serious mischief, and then proceeded to the mill of Messrs Titley, Tatham and Walker, Water Lane, which they were engaged in stopping when Prince George with the Lancers came up at full speed and formed in a line in Camp Field. The riot act was read, and two or three of the ringleaders were taken prisoners.

All rather unfortunate because Marshall was one of the pioneers of workers' safety and education and did much to mitigate the dangers inherent in running and working in a textile mill. He was only too aware of the flammability of textiles and so built twenty-five fire escapes into his building; multi-storey spelled death trap with carnage and mayhem a possibility on stairways so he made temple Works single storey. Like Rowntree, Titus Salt and Cadbury he felt a social responsibility towards his workers and their families: the undercroft housed children's dormitories, shops, doctors, a church; there was a school adjacent to the mill at ground level. The children, until aged twelve, were well looked after while their parents worked to bring home the bacon.

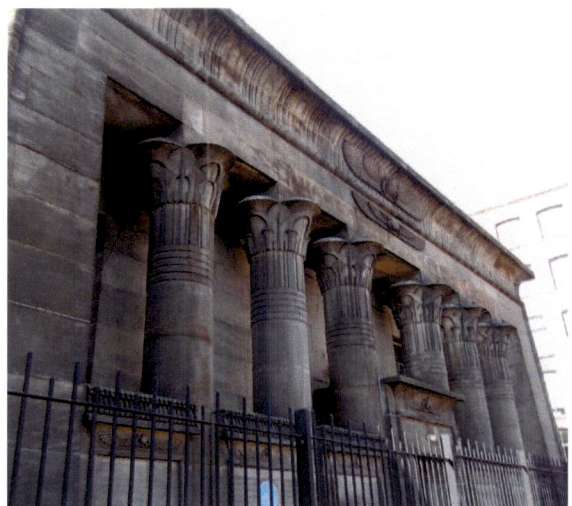

Another shot of Joseph Bonomi the Younger's Leeds temple showing the magnificent columns and capitals.

15. The Dark Arches (1846), Granary Wharf

One of the most significant changes in Leeds in the latter half of the nineteenth century was caused by the coming of the railway to the city and the construction of Wellington Station and New Station over the river and the northern part of the Canal Basin. Wellington Station dates from 1846; between 1866 and 1869 the North Eastern Railway constructed the New Station to connect lines from Bradford and the west and lines to York, Selby and the North East.

The station was, amazingly, built over a series of arches, spanning the Aire, Neville Street and Swinegate. This magnificent edifice – the Dark Arches – can still be seen and enjoyed today. More than eighteen million bricks were used in their construction, a record at the time in what was a series of independent viaducts two or four tracks wide. The station is at the terminus of the Leeds and Liverpool Canal, but as it is raised high above ground level you can access the Dark Arches from the towpath.

At first, the arches were used for storage, some of them by soap manufacturers Joseph Watson & Sons, to store resin, oil and tallow. Unfortunately, in 1892 these inventories and the bridge and railway line over the canal basin were destroyed in a fire. The bridge was rebuilt, and the line restored in just five-and-a-half days.

Joseph Watson & Sons and their Whitehall Soap Works was one of the largest soap works in England, employing around 750 people, and manufacturing 600 tons of soap a week in 1893. Famous brands included Watson's Matchless Cleanser, and Venus Soap; the firm was known as Soapy Joe's. They also made glycerine for dynamite production, and traded in hides and skins. Watson's was sold to Lever's in 1917, and became Elida Gibbs in 1971, closing in 1987 when the company moved to Seacroft.

The Dark Arches is now part of Granary Wharf, with shops, restaurants, markets and street entertainers.

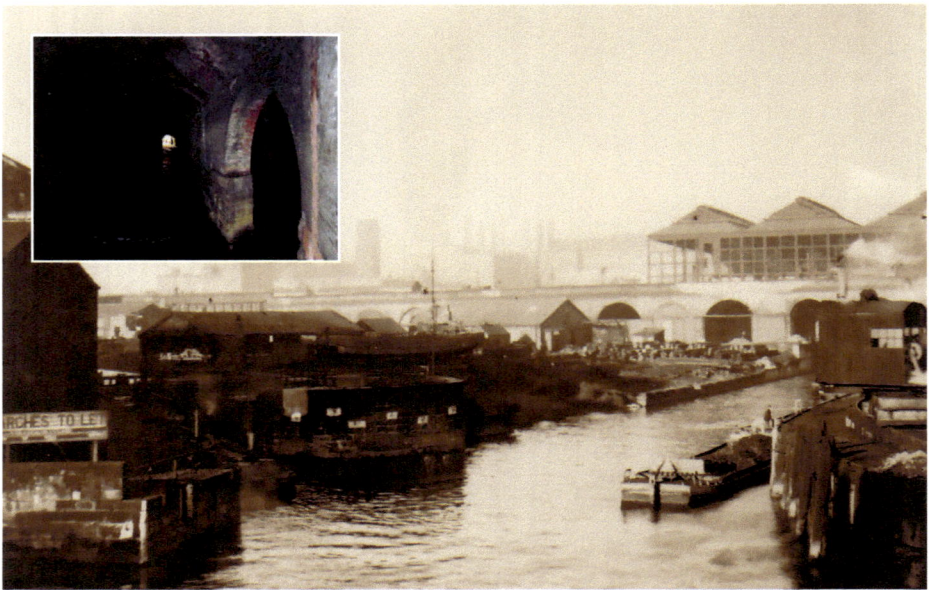

Arches to let on a commercial and industrial Leeds and (*inset*) light at the end of the tunnel in the very dark vaults.

16. HM Prison Leeds (1847), Gloucester Terrace, Stanningley Road, Armley

HM Prison Leeds is a category-B men's prison which opened in 1847 and is still referred to locally as Armley Gaol. The suitably grim-looking building was built from locally quarried stone with four wings radiating from a central point, each of which had three landings of cells – on the 'then modern penitentiary principal with four radial wings'. It was responsible for incarcerating prisoners sentenced in the West Riding but also took over the gruesome task of executing West Riding prisoners from York Castle. Ninety three men and one woman suffered the death penalty at Armley between 1864 and 1961 – an average of almost one every year. Hungarian Zsiga Pankotia was the last to swing, courtesy of Harry Allen, in 1961 for the murder of Jack Eli Myers for a house burglary in Roundhay.

Two new wings were added in 1994 and a new gate complex opened in September 2002. The prison can accommodate up to 1,212 prisoners in 551 normal cells and in six residential units, a segregation unit, First Night Centre, Vulnerable Prisoner unit and inpatients Healthcare Facility.

The website capitalpunishment.org recounts three particularly disturbing executions:

> There was to be only one public execution outside the jail – a double hanging on 10 September 1864. It was of murderers James Sargisson and Joseph Myers. Myers had tried to cheat the hangman by cutting his throat while in prison but was saved by the surgeon. The hangings were reported in detail by The *Leeds Mercury* newspaper

which claimed that between 80,000 to 100,000 people had come to watch the event on that Saturday morning. At five minutes to nine, the prison bell began to toll and inside the two men were being pinioned by Thomas Askern of York. They were led out onto the gallows supported on each side by warders and preceded by the Under Sheriff and the Chaplain. Askern pulled down the white caps over their faces but both men continued to speak, Sargisson's last words to Myers were reportedly 'Art thou happy lad?' to which Myers responded 'Indeed I am.' Askern then operated the drop which fell with a thud, their bodies being almost completely hidden from the crowd. Myers seemed to die almost immediately, but Sargisson struggled for some minutes. As feared the wound in Myers' throat had reopened and there was an amount of blood on his shirt. After hanging the customary hour, they were removed from the gallows and buried within the prison.

Botched executions were not uncommon at this time and 'a shocking scene' was reported by the *Yorkshire Post* newspaper following the hanging of thirty-seven-year-old John Henry Johnson on Wednesday the 3 April 1877. Johnson had been condemned for the murder of Amos Waite who had been showing interest in Johnson's wife Amelia on Boxing Day 1876. After a drunken quarrel in the pub where they were all drinking, Johnson went home, returning a little while later with a gun and shooting Waite in the chest. Thomas Askern was called to Leeds to dispatch Johnson and had made the usual preparations on the Tuesday afternoon but when he pulled the lever the rope broke and Johnson plummeted through the trap. He was immediately rescued by the warders who removed his straps and hood and sat him on a chair. It took Askern ten minutes to rig a new rope and reset the trap before Johnson could again be led up onto it. This time the rope held but it was reported that Johnson 'died hard' struggling for some four minutes on the rope. His death was formally recorded as being from asphyxia but no official mention was made of the failure of first attempt to hang him. It was to be Askern's last execution at Armley.

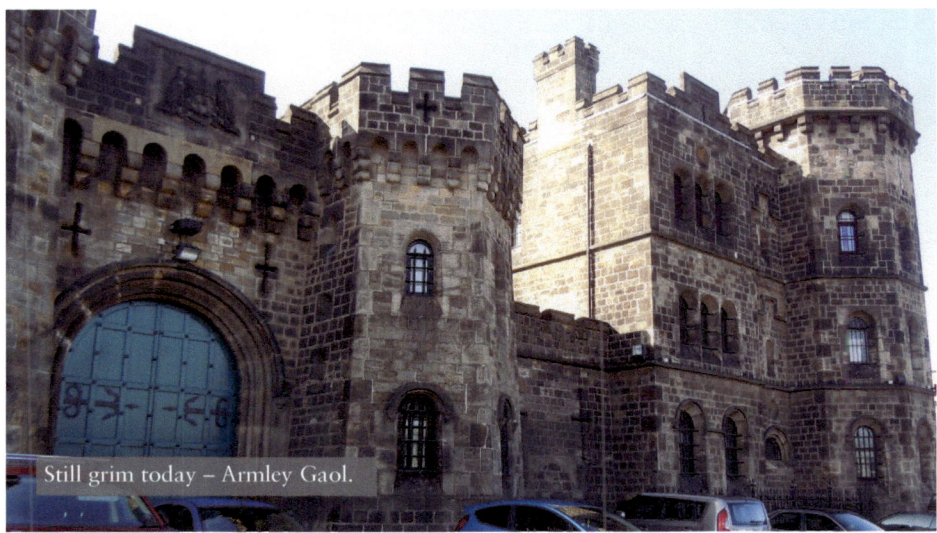

Still grim today – Armley Gaol.

17. City Varieties (1857), Swan Street, The Headrow

City Varieties began life in 1760 when the White Swan Coaching Inn was built in a yard off Briggate, appropriately known as the White Swan Yard. The White Swan featured a singing room upstairs, where various acts, though not drama, were staged. Charles Thornton became the licensee of the White Swan in 1857 and, after refurbishment, reopened in 1865 as 'Thornton's New Music Hall and Fashionable Lounge' – big enough to hold audiences of 2,000 or so. It remains a rare surviving example of Victorian era music halls of the 1850s and 1860s. A contemporary review says 'billiards and supper rooms were attached, and the place was noted for its attentive waiters'.

Thornton's New Music Hall was one of many successful Leeds venues. These also included the Rose and Crown on Briggate and the Princess Palace Music Hall which reopened in 1874 after refurbishment. Thornton leased the White Swan to John Stansfield, and went on to build Thornton's Arcade. In 1880 Stansfield changed the name to Stansfield's Varieties and then in the early 1890s the theatre was bought by Thomas Dunford, who changed the name again to Leeds City Varieties Music Hall. In the face of competition from the new Empire Theatre in Briggate in 1898 the theatre was sold to Fred Wood, who booked acts such as Charlie Chaplin, starring as one of 'The Eight Lancashire Lads', Lily Langtry, George Formby senior, Laurel and Hardy, and Chirgwin, who was billed as 'The White Eyed Kaffir'. Houdini appeared there in 1904; he was paid £130.18s 6d (around £7,500 in today's money – the most anyone had ever been paid to appear on stage at a theatre). When Lily Langtry performed there, Edward VII would surreptitiously go in to see her. In gratitude for the theatre's discretion he donated the crest which is now displayed above the auditorium.

In September 1913 and in March 1915 the theatre offered a challenge to local men to compete in wrestling matches. The Christmas pantomime of 1941, aptly *Babes in the Wood*, featured some unique audience participation when a woman (unexpectedly) gave birth to a 'healthy ginger-haired boy'. Harry Joseph, the owner, gave the baby boy free admission to the Varieties for life.

When the Luftwaffe bombed the Argyll Theatre in Birkenhead, the City Varieties was left as Britain's oldest surviving music hall. Less conventional performances at Leeds included the lady who hypnotised an alligator to a musical accompaniment. It was Harry Joseph who discovered Frankie Ableson, who went on to become Frankie Vaughan. In the 1950s Joseph put on striptease shows in which the girls were allowed to pose (salaciously presumably), but not to move, . 1953 saw the start of the BBC's *The Good Old Days* which ran for thirty years.

Through the 1970s and 1980s, the striptease shows were abandoned in a return to family entertainment and the theatre put on variety shows, reviews, and drama; it was sold to Leeds City Council, who leased it to Leeds Grand Theatre and Opera House Ltd. The theatre reopened in September 2011 after a major refurbishment with seating for 467. 'If you wanted to wear your top hat you'd go to the Grand, but if you wanted to wear your flat cap you'd go to the City Varieties.'

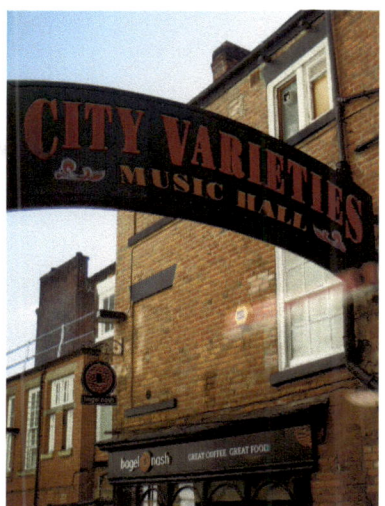

City Varieties Music Hall, Swan Street, named after the White Swan Inn – still the good old days.

18. Leeds Town Hall (1858), The Headrow

The town hall is a symbol of the grandeur that was Victorian Leeds, built on Park Lane, now the Headrow. It was an expression of civic pride and a reflection of the wealth brought to the city by the textile industries.

Before the town hall, until 1813, the moot hall, which had stood in the middle of Briggate, had performed the city's civic and judicial function from 1615. It was rebuilt in 1710/11, with a gable featuring a statue of Queen Anne. A pillory and

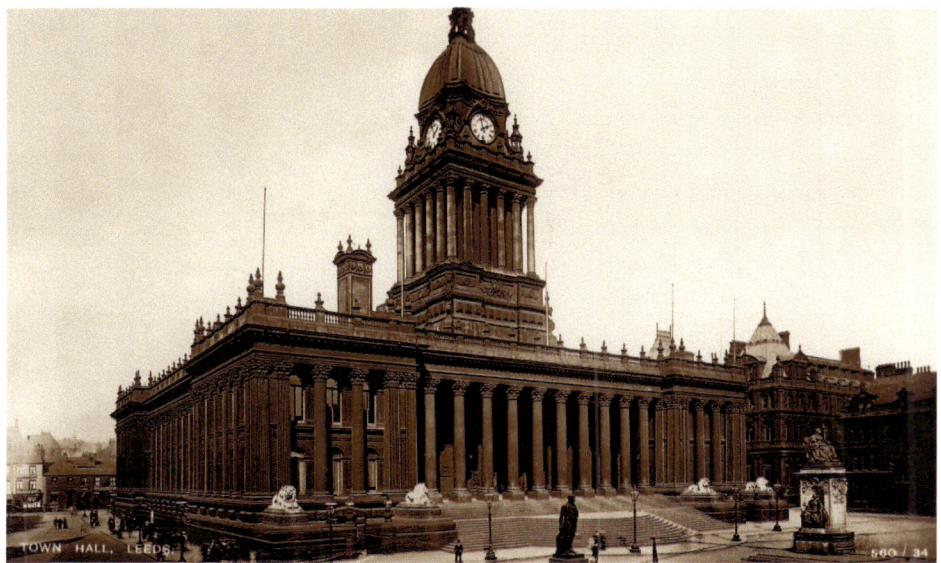

A fine photograph of the town hall in 1912.

stocks stood in front of the building as a caution to all. But with the rise in the city's population the moot proved inadequate so a new courthouse was built. The moot hall found itself somewhat redundant as a result and was demolished in 1825. The courthouse took over the role of general post office when the town hall opened.

It was home to a number of municipal departments, a courtroom, a police station otherwise known as 'central charge office', comprising a police muster room, thirteen prison cells, known as the Bridewell, and accommodation for the jailer and his wife.

Bridewell is the name for a town lock-up – a small remand prison used to house prisoners awaiting their appearance in court. The name comes from a prison for vagrants and petty offenders in London, near the church of St Brides and close to a well, hence Bridewell.

Each cell comprised a wooden bench, shackle rings for wrists and ankles fastened to the bench and the wall, stone-flagged floors, whitewashed walls, and no windows. According to the 'Bridewell Charter' each prisoner 'should have half a loaf of bread and a pint of ale together with sufficient straw for bedding'. Each cell held up to four prisoners, who would have been cold and very cramped. The 'cooler cells' were reserved for violent and intoxicated offenders – open to the elements with bars as windows.

Grandest of all, though, was a venue for concerts and civic functions, the ornate Victoria Hall – 92 feet high, 161 feet long and 72 feet wide it was big enough to

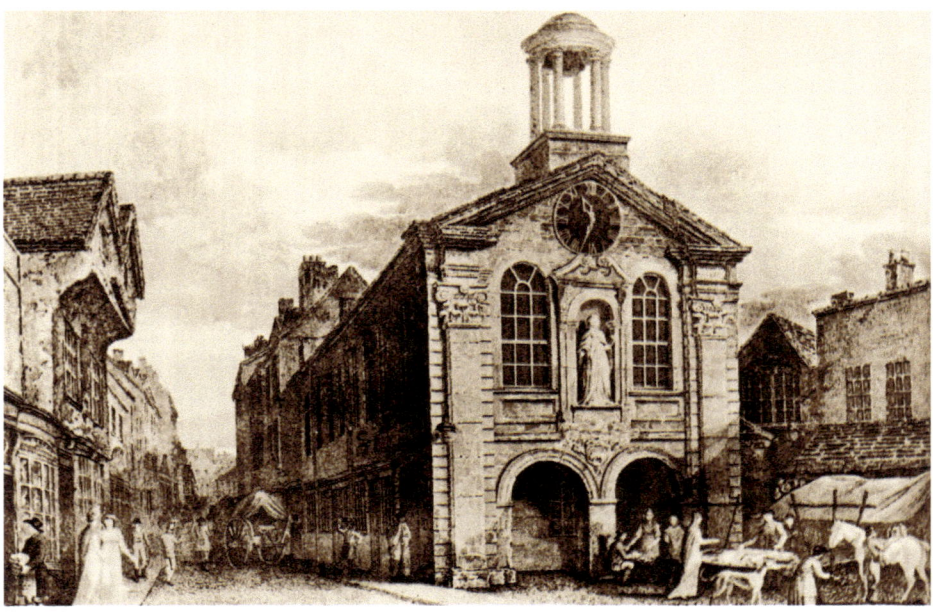

The moot hall in Briggate which preceded the town hall. The moot hall was a seventeenth-century building which has since been demolished. A statue of Queen Anne formally occupied the niche, it is now in the City Art Gallery.

seat 8,000 people. *The Intelligencer* of 11 September 1858 reports that the hall 'was enriched with colour in an almost lavish manner, every portion being more or less decorated'. Its concert organ is the largest three-manual example in Europe. The organ was built by Gray and Davison, whose workshop had to be enlarged in order to build it. The swell box was the largest they had ever built – a dinner party was held inside the box at the factory.

During the Second World War an ARP post operated from the basement and from 1942 a British restaurant opened there, also known as the Civic Restaurant; it was refurbished in 1960 and closed in 1966. In 2000 the Central Library in the civic hall was extensively renovated. During this time the library was housed in the crypt. Books were stored in the basement, some in the cells of the Bridewell.

Nowadays, it is the venue for the Leeds International Pianoforte Competition, the Leeds International Film Festival screenings and the Leeds International Beer Festival. At 225 feet it was Leeds' tallest building from 1858 until 1966, when it lost out to the Park Plaza Hotel, which was 26 feet taller. It held this title longer than any other building in the city: 108 years. The striking clock tower was added by architect Brodrick to enhance further the grandeur of the building. In 1933 Leeds Civic Hall took over the municipal role of the town hall.

In November 2008, *Architecture Today* said of the town hall:

> The epitome of northern civic bombast, Leeds' municipal palace has a grandeur that helps sustain the city's sense of its own importance. Its architect, Cuthbert Broderick, also contributed the Corn Exchange and City Museum before disappearing into obscurity.

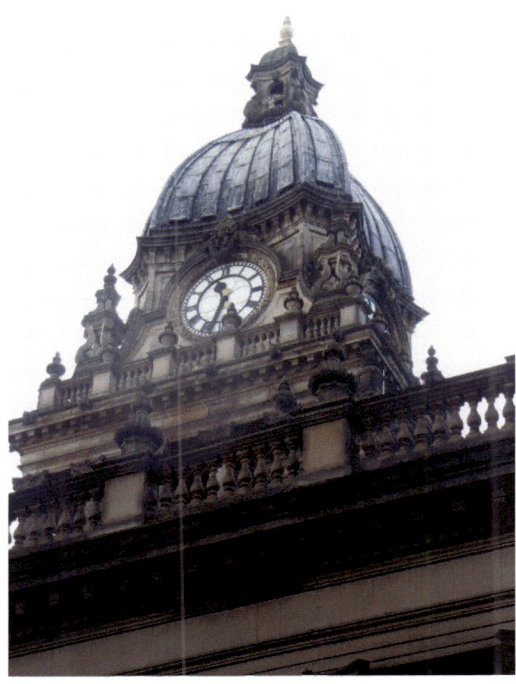

The clock at 11.35 a.m., 26 September 2015.

19. The Corn Exchange (1864), Call Lane

Corn has been formally traded in Leeds since the seventeenth century when the corn market was at the top of Briggate, between the Market Cross and New Street (now New Briggate). In 1827, growing trade led to the building of a corn exchange at the top of Briggate, but by the mid-nineteenth century this too proved too small.

So, in 1860, a new corn exchange was proposed, to be designed and built along the lines of the state-of-the-art Edinburgh Corn Exchange. The Edinburgh exchange featured a large central space, in effect a trading floor, where farmers and corn factors transacted their business. The version at Leeds featured a large central space surrounded by fifty-six offices, accessed by arched doorways, some of them opened onto the street, while others opened into the interior of the building. Corn was stored in the huge basement area. It was also used as the headquarters of the fire brigade for a while.

Leeds Corn Exchange is one of just three corn exchanges in the country which still retain their original function as marketplaces, although not in the buying and selling of corn anymore. The building was a centre for the sale of corn wheat, barley, hops, peas, beans, seeds, oil cake and flour and hosted a farmers market and a regular leather fair.

When it closed there were proposals to turn it into a northern Albert Hall but it was converted into a retail centre of some considerable splendour and reopened in 1990. The sympathetic renovation retained most of the original furnishings: merchants' desks, sample trays, and name boards.

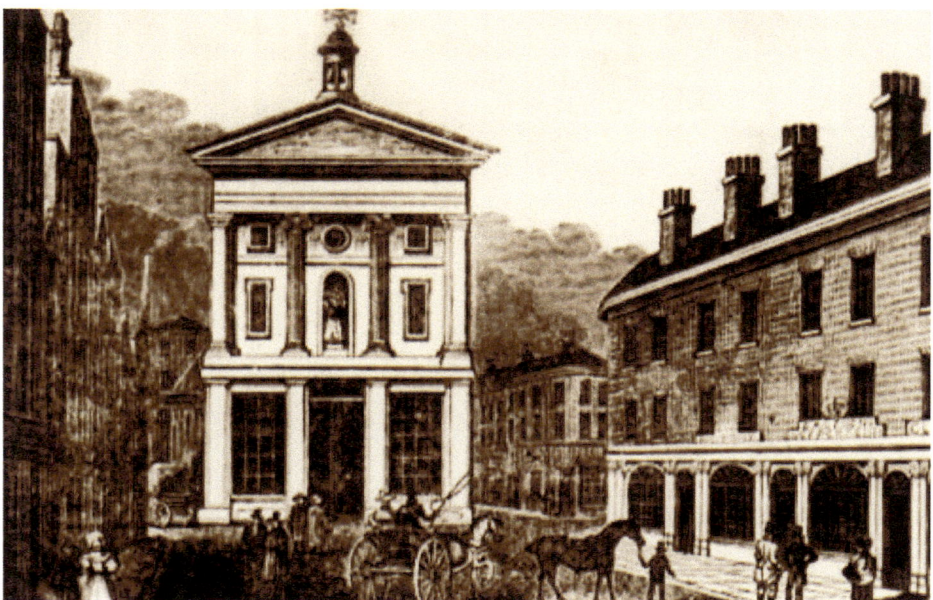

The original 1827 Leeds Corn Exchange at the top of Briggate, between the Market Cross and New Street, now New Briggate.

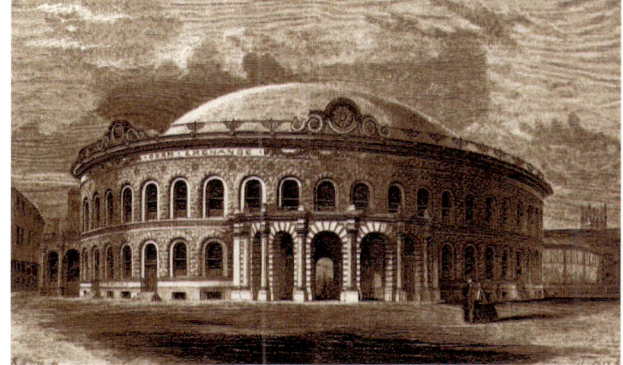

The corn exchange on the outside, soon after its opening, and modelled on the exchange at Edinburgh, published in *The Builder* journal in 1861.

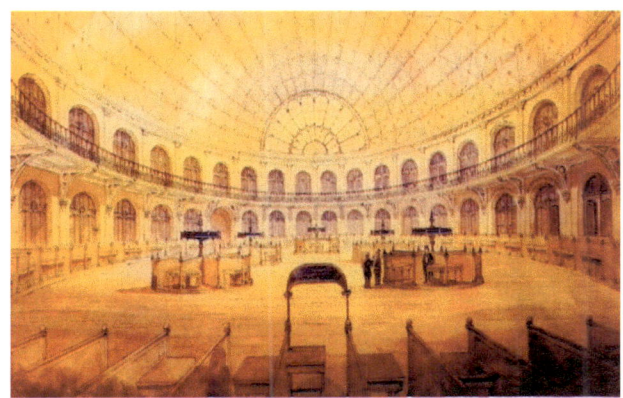

The interior of the corn exchange giving a good impression of the huge dome and trading floor.

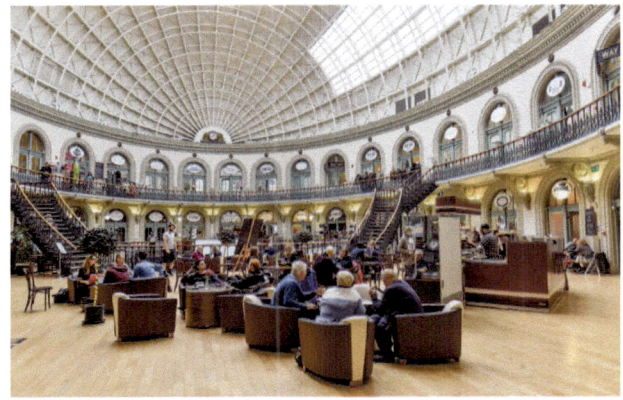

A busy corn exchange today. (Courtesy of Leeds Corn Exchange)

2c. Tower Works (1864), Globe Road, Holbeck

Tower Works was founded by T. R. Harding in 1829; he moved it to this site in the early 1860s. Harding, a lover of all things Italian, was one of Britain's great inventors, but he is rarely recognised as such. His firm made steel pins for use in the textile industry; the Harding gauge was the recognised international standard classification system for pin sizes. The factory also made measuring instruments, while the 'Ideal Counter' could count the number of items a machine turned out, or could record production, for example of textiles or paper, in units of length. Harding tachometers, or speed indicators, were used on marine and stationary engines, and also in manufacturing to measure the number of units made in a given time.

The factory was situated south of the Leeds–Liverpool canal west of the Canal Basin and was called Tower Works on account of its three magnificent towers, built in the style of an Italian campanile. The smaller tower from 1864 is a copy of the twelfth-century campanile at the Palazzo del Comune in Verona, and was built as a chimney. The larger tower was built in 1899 to resemble Giotto's iconic 1334 campanile in Florence; its industrial purpose was to extract the fine metal dust produced during the manufacturing process. A third, plain tower, built in 1919, represents a Tuscan tower house. The Engine Room is currently used for art exhibitions and installations. Many of the wonderful original features have been retained, 'including a mosaic floor in red, black and white abstract patterns and a series of circular glazed bronze plaques, each featuring a portrait connected with the manufacture of textile machinery' (tower-works.com).

Col T. W. Harding, the son of the founder of the firm, had an invaluable influence on Leeds' cultural and civic life: he was a co-founder of the City Art Gallery, to which he donated several paintings, and he gifted the statues which now stand proudly in City Square: the Black Prince, Dean Hook, Joseph Priestly and the

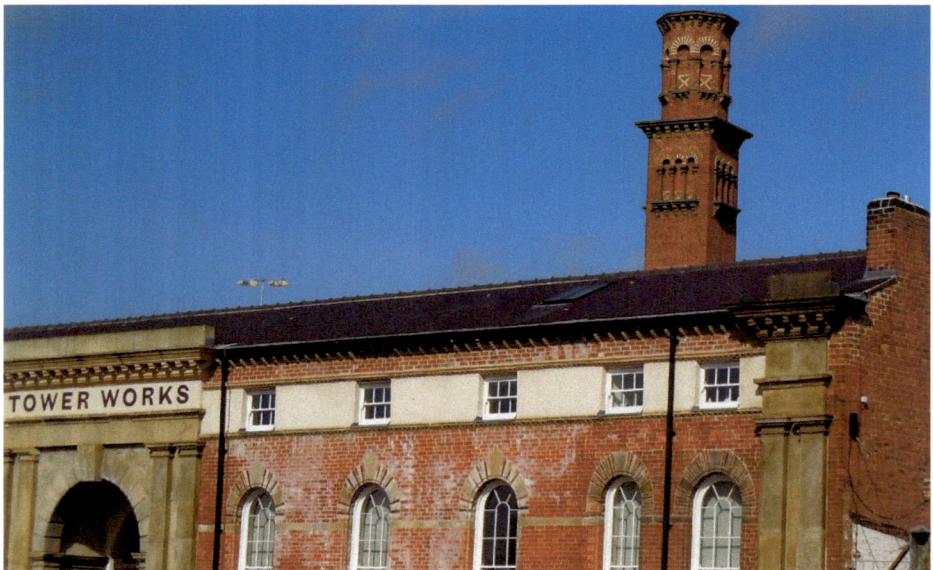

Tower Works bringing a touch of Renaissance Italy to Victorian Leeds. This one was inspired by the Torre dei Lamberti in Verona where the two bells have two very important functions: the Marangona alerts the people of fires, work times, and the hours of the day; the Rengo calls the population to arms or invokes the city's councils.

figures of 'Morn' and 'Even'. He was colonel of the Leeds Artillery Volunteers and was the first lord mayor of Leeds in 1898/9 and president of the Leeds Chamber of Commerce. He lived in and refurbished Abbey House, now the museum at Kirkstall Abbey.

The firm became Harding Richardson, Rhodes & Co. Ltd around 1895 and then from 1919 it was known as Harding Rhodes & Co. Ltd, which remained its name until 1981. Tower Works is now part of Holbeck Urban Village and provides office space for small businesses.

21. The Griffin (1872), Boar Lane

The Grade II-listed Griffin on Boar Lane was previously known as Bar Censsa and before that The Griffin Hotel, one of the top hotels in Leeds; it closed in 1999. The Gothic Revival building boasted a unique Potts clock at its corner with the hours ingeniously replaced by the words 'Griffin Hotel'. For many, though, the Griffin will be cherished as the place where Leeds United was born. The pub is on the site of the earlier Griffin Hotel, a coaching inn from at least the seventeenth century. It was rebuilt as a railway hotel, for the Leeds New Station which opened in 1869, owned by the joint London & North West and North East Railways.

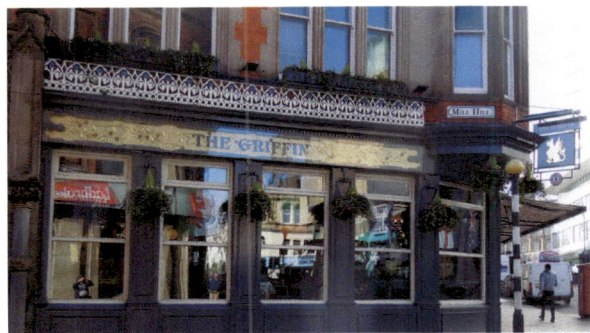

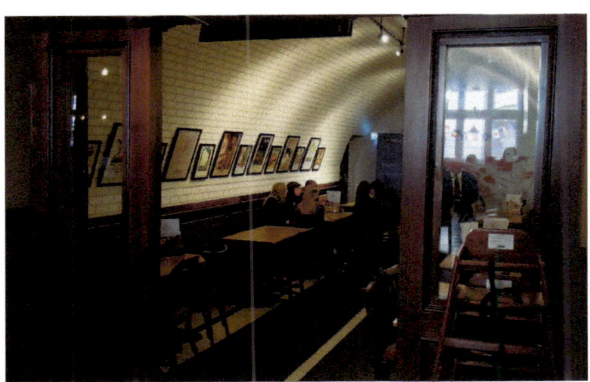

The Griffin pub – elegant exterior and atmospheric interior.

22. Kirkgate Market (1875), Vicar Lane

As we have seen, Leeds was always a market town trading one commodity or another. Defoe observed that the cloth market was a swift, early morning affair starting at 7.00 a.m. and all over by 9.00 a.m. when it was time for a good breakfast taken at public houses near the bridge. These meals were called Brig-End-Shots which, according to Ralph Thoresby, 'the clothier may, together with his Pot of Ale, have a Noggin o' Pottage, and a Trencher of either Boil'd or Roast Beef for two Pence'.

At 9.00 a.m. the general traders set up and took over. Thoresby again gives us the details as they were in 1715:

> the market people of other professions, as Country Linen Drapers, Shoo-makers, hardware men, and the sellers of Wood Vessels, Wicker Basket, Wanded Chairs, Flakes [fences] etc.; the fruit sellers both wholesale and retail; the farmers selling dairy cattle; the fish traders; the butchers in the Shambles behind the Moot Hall; the egg, butter and poultry sellers; and the corn traders.

Up to 500 loads of apples might be sold in one day. There was a cattle market; the fish market was 'furnished with a great variety of fish'. The butchers' shambles remained on one side of the moot hall, with the wool market on the other. The poultry market was at the cross above the moot hall while above this was the corn market. There was also a horse fair in the Upper Headrow while the pig market was in the Lower Headrow, and the corn market was between the Market Cross and New Street. In other parts of the town, Thoresby concludes, there sold 'whatever is necessary for the comfortable Sustenance of Mankind, though too tedious particularly to recite'.

Leeds markets usually means Kirkgate Market but there were other market buildings, such as the Central Market and the South Market, established in the 1820s. Between 1600 and 1800 the cloth market moved from Briggate to the Cloth Halls although Briggate remained the site of the general market. Briggate was by

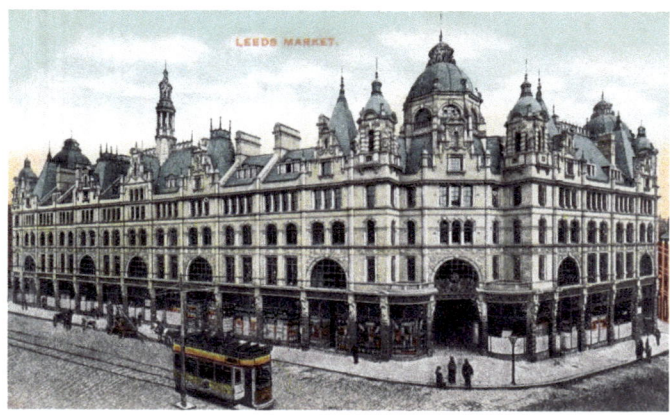

Leeds markets in the 1920s.

now a busy main road and quite an unsuitable place for a market. Something had to be done but the traders, shopkeepers and innkeepers could not agree on a site. Accordingly, between 1823 and 1829, no fewer than five different markets were built, including Kirkgate, which started life as an open-air market on Vicar's Croft in 1822. Around 1875 Kirkgate became a covered market. Leeds New Market was built, catering for general produce and fish and a new fish market, an abattoir and a meat market were built later. In the early years of the twentieth century, the old covered market was demolished and replaced by the grand new market hall.

The Bazaar and Shambles, between Briggate and Vicar Lane, was established in 1825 by two well-named butchers, Frederick and Joseph Rinder. On the ground floor there were sixty stalls, fifty of which were butchers, arranged in two streets. On the first floor was the bazaar – a block of shops which was let to dealers for the sale of fancy goods, millinery and clothes. In 1858 part of the bazaar was used as a carpet warehouse. The building was bought in 1898 by Leeds Corporation and demolished to make way for a new road.

The South Market was built in Meadow Lane in 1824 as a general retail market. It comprised twenty-three butchers, twenty-six other shops, eighty-eight stalls, nine slaughter houses and eighteen houses. But the South Market failed and from 1827 only quarterly leather fairs were held there, and it became known as the leather market.

The Central Market was a covered market in Duncan Street from 1827. Most of the shops were butchers and fishmongers, although the covered central space had stalls for fruit, vegetables, and dairy produce. There was also a balcony where fancy goods were sold. In total it contained sixty-seven shops, fifty-six stalls, six offices and a hotel. As with South Market it was never a great success; Leeds Corporation bought it in 1868. The building was badly damaged by fire in 1893, and was knocked down with the extension of Vicar Lane into Duncan Street.

We have seen that a corn exchange was built at the top of Briggate in 1827. It had warehouses and offices for the use of corn factors, a hotel, an inn and four shops.

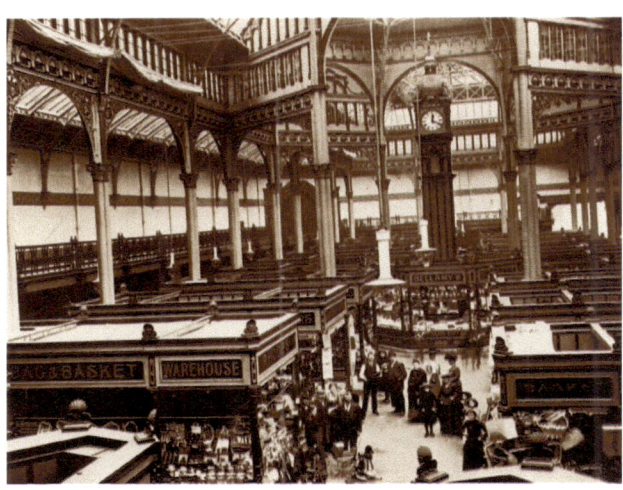

Inside Leeds markets.

Despite it all, there was still no wholesale fruit and vegetable market or indeed a cattle market. An obvious site for another market was Vicar's Croft. The cow and pig market had already moved there in 1822, along with the fish market and the wholesale fruit and vegetable market.

Kirkgate Market, as it was called, was a great success, but since no tolls were paid, there was no money to pay for the upkeep of the market or to clear the rubbish and filth that piled up. From 1830, tolls were exacted and improvements were made. Soon there was a need for a larger market. The council bought the adjacent land and the market extension was completed in 1846, housing the cattle market and the fruit and vegetable market. In 1855 the cattle market moved to between North Street and Camp Road, where twice-yearly horse and cattle fairs were also held.

Weather was a major problem: the market was duly covered over and opened in May 1857 à la Crystal Palace: The *Leeds Guide* of 1858 gives us the details:

> The building is of iron and glass, covering an area of 4,040 yards and is situate at the junction of Vicar Lane and Kirkgate. The style of architecture is Gothic. It has forty-four convenient shops on the outside, and thirty-five inside, where there are also four rows of iron stalls. At night this beautiful crystal market hall is well illuminated by 200 gaslights, arranged round handsome cast-iron pillars. Altogether it is the most complete structure of its kind in England.

It sold everything from 'Poultry to Potatoes; Books to Nuts; Images to Mercery, and Bacon to Beans.' Dogs, hawkers, smoking, and swearing were banned. Kirkgate Market was expanded again in 1875, and Leeds New Market was built. A new covered pig market for up to 1,500 pigs was built, with space for a hay and straw market. At the New Market the fish market was in a square with its cleaning central fountain. There were five rows of retail fruit and vegetable shops and the Game and the egg and butter market and an area where dogs

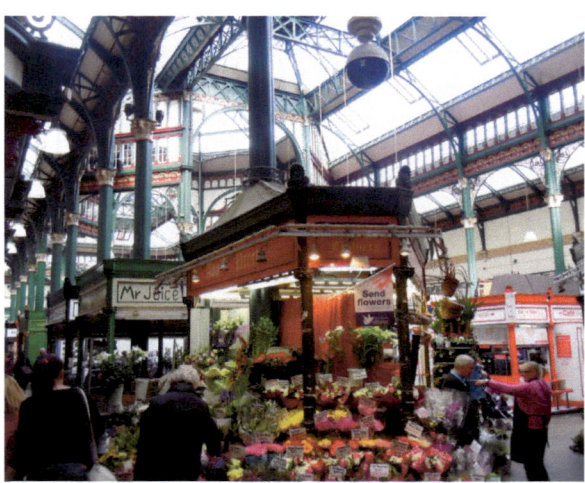

Leeds markets in all their glory; the 2015 photograph illustrates just how rewarding it is to look up at the roof now and again. The site of Marks & Spencer's Penny Bazaar can also be seen in the modern photograph.

and birds were sold. In 1884, Marks of Marks & Spencer opened a stall in the market: their original penny bazaar. Michael Marks was an immigrant Lithuanian Jew who began trading with a penny bazaar store where everything cost a penny: the nineteenth-century equivalent of today's pound shop. He later moved to Wigan where he teamed up with Tom Spencer of Skipton to form what was to become one of the most enduring and successful British retailing companies.

Kirkgate Market is still one of the largest in Europe with some 800 stalls and 100,000 people visiting the market on Saturdays, attracting shoppers from as far away as Newcastle, Hull and Sheffield.

23. Leeds University Union (1877), Woodhouse Lane

The history and development of the Union roughly follows the development of the university it is associated with. Today's union has its origins with the various societies of the Yorkshire College which joined the federal Victoria University in 1887; the Yorkshire College Students Association was the first such society. Rooms and areas within university buildings, which then were mainly converted town houses, were used as common rooms and meeting spaces for the students until 1937 when work began on the current university union building built big enough to hold 2,000 students. Completed in 1939, it was extended in the 1960s and again in the late 1990s to accommodate a student population of 24,000.

The Union today features three nightclubs: Stylus, Pulse and Mine, which are used as concert venues, with the university's adjoining Refectory, deployed for larger events. It was here that The Who recorded Live at Leeds in 1970 – one of the best live albums of all time; other acts over the years have included Bob Marley and the Wailers, as heard on the remastered 2004 'Burnin', Jimi Hendrix, Led Zeppelin, Pink Floyd, and more recently, Muse, Manic Street Preachers, KT Tunstall, Arctic Monkeys and Paul Weller.

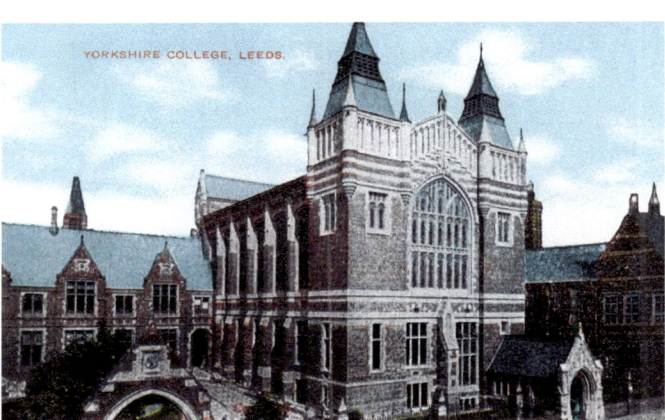

The original Yorkshire College, now part of the University of Leeds.

24. Grand Theatre (1878), New Briggate

The Leeds Grand Theatre and Opera House opened in 1878, according to the website, as 'a backlash to the music hall tradition which was thought by "polite society" to lower the tone of entertainment via the sort of humour presented in these pub-based establishments'. No doubt the working-class City Varieties was very much in mind.

The catalyst was back in 1858 when Victoria and Albert visited Leeds to open the new town hall. Albert observed that 'Leeds seemed in need of a good theatre, and that nothing was more calculated to promote the culture and raise the tone of the people'. In 1875 the Theatre Royal in Hunslet Lane was razed by fire, followed by the Amphitheatre in 1876. Something had to be done, so a company was formed that year to construct a new theatre for Leeds; it was to be housed in a Gothic-style building which included assembly rooms and six shops.

Much of the design had foreign influences, including the Gothic, church-influenced spires, Romanesque and Scottish Baronial touches. Only those people with tickets for the best seats were allowed to use the theatre's main entrance; there was however, a 'transfer staircase' which enabled anyone in the audience to improve on their position by paying more. The dress circle and boxes contained free-standing chairs, but all other parts had benches of varying comfort according to price. Packers were hired to shoehorn in the people sitting on these wooden benches. It is, by common consent, a triumph of Victorian theatre building: the scene dock here has one of the most complete, still-functioning Victorian scenic paint shops left in the country.

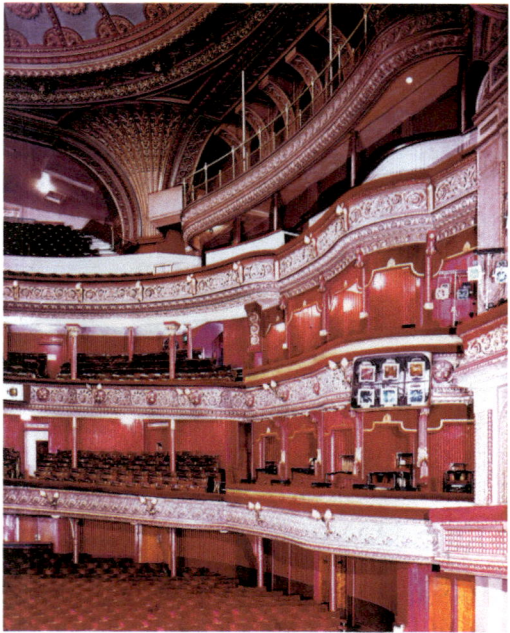

Inside the plush Grand Theatre showing the four levels of seating area and part of the ornate ceiling. (Courtesy of Leodis, © Leeds Library & Information Services)

The premier performance was *Much Ado About Nothing* on 18 November 1878 with Kirkstall Abbey as backdrop. Over the years stars who performed there have included Sarah Bernhardt in 1881, Ellen Terry in 1882, Henry Irving, Julie Andrews, Felicity Kendal, Morecambe and Wise and Laurence Olivier.

The theatre held 2,600 people, with standing room for 200 more. Lessons were learnt from the earlier theatre fires: Wilson Barrett, the confident manager, promised that 'If the stage were engulfed by fire, every gentleman would have time to light his cigar comfortably, give his arm to his lady love, and saunter pleasantly out of the building.' The theatre was lit by 400 gas jets. In the event of these causing a fire, water could be substituted for gas in the 15 miles of gas piping, and ejected through the gas jets. Dressing rooms were heated by gas pipes; miles of speaking tubes provided communication between various parts of the theatre.

Barrett's contract must have been challenging for him: he had to pay £1,700 rent per year, and although the theatre expensed up to £800 for scenery, Barrett had to pay for the props.

The Grand also serves an opera house, and in 1913 Thomas Beecham, with the Denhof Opera Company, presented Wagner's complete *Ring of the Niebelung*; the D'Oyly Carte Opera Company put on six Gilbert and Sullivan operas in one week in 1912. In ballet, Anna Pavlova made three visits to the Grand Theatre around 1912. In November 1977 the theatre became home to Opera North, whose first performance was *Samson and Delilah* by Camille Saint-Saëns.

25. Thornton's Arcade (1878), Victoria Quarter – off Briggate

The buildings and conditions in what was to become the beautiful Victoria Quarter could not have been more different before 1877. Vicar Lane was full of slaughterhouses, butchers, fruit and vegetable stalls, while at the western end of County Arcade was the Bazaar, a two-storey emporium – the lower level selling meat and the upper level fancy goods and haberdashery. Men and women were segregated – men downstairs, women upstairs – with no chatting, no drinking or eating behind the counters and no bonnet-wearing by the women.

This was before the famous theatre architect Frank Matcham was commissioned to redevelop the area. Matcham could, by then, put his name to more than 200 theatres and music halls, including the London Palladium and Coliseum. For the new Victoria Arcade he used opulent marbles, gilded mosaics, imposing cast and wrought iron, as well as carved and polished mahogany, to create two streets, an arcade and the Empire Theatre, which was demolished in the 1960s – Harvey Nichols occupies the site now.

Highlights (literally) are Brian Clarke's breathtaking stained-glass roof, extending the full length of Queen Victoria Street and the largest stained-glass window in Britain – at 746.9 square metres – and three splendid mosaic floor panels by Joanna Veevers in County Arcade. The original ornate mahogany frames survived the dilapidation and the gilded art nouveau lettering has been restored.

The refurbished Queen Victoria Street with its coloured roof stretching the 400 feet from one end of the street to the other: still the largest single work of stained glass in Great Britain. 'Visitors to the Victoria Quarter are treated to an unforgettable coloured sky. Even during grey autumn afternoons the glass vivifies the space' (brianclarke.co.uk).

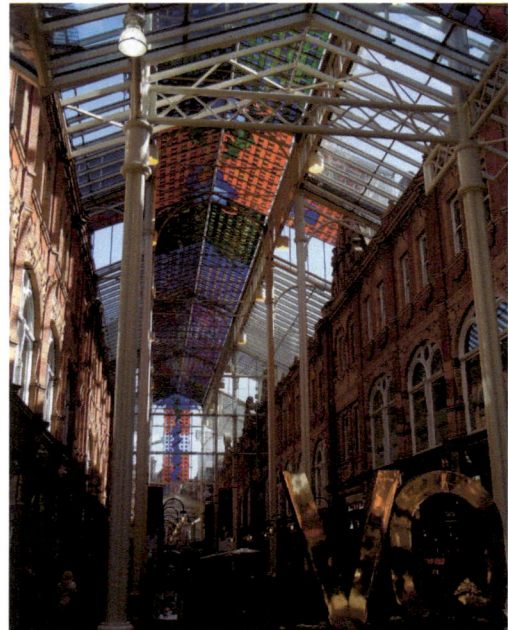

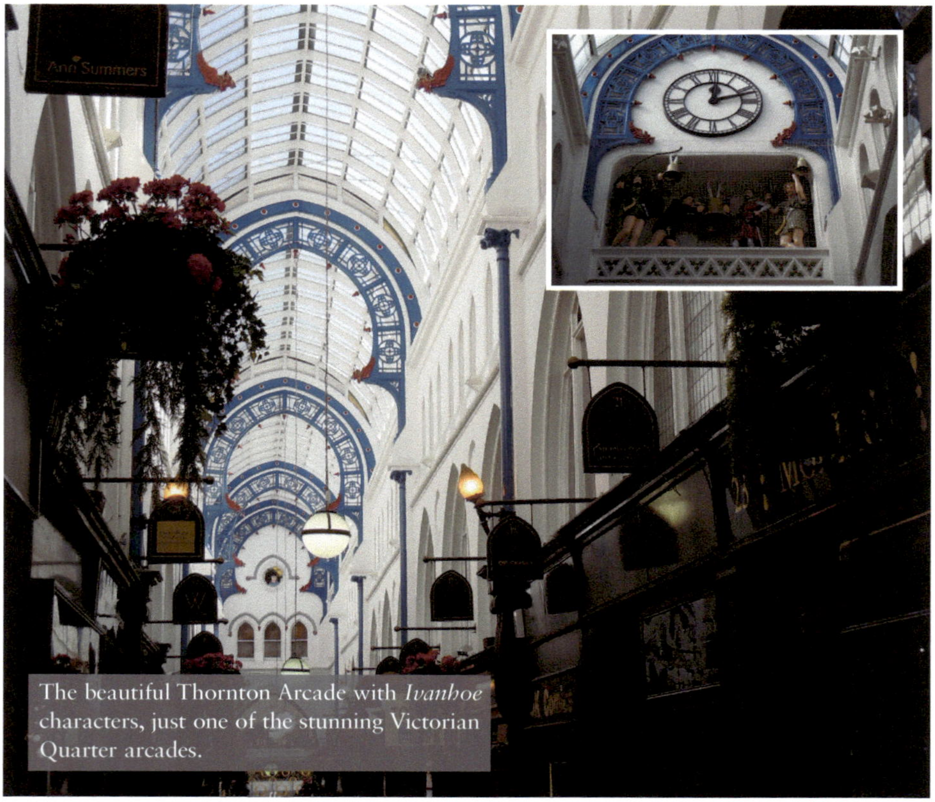

The beautiful Thornton Arcade with *Ivanhoe* characters, just one of the stunning Victorian Quarter arcades.

Thornton's three-storey arcade was the first to open in 1878, named after Charles Thornton. The arcade is famous for its clock, made by William Potts & Sons of Leeds, which features animated life-sized characters from Sir Walter Scott's *Ivanhoe*. Robin Hood and Gurth the Swineherd strike the quarter hours; Friar Tuck and Richard the Lionheart strike the hours. At the other end of the arcade is a woman's head, sporting long curling hair and a large hat. It is modelled on Gainsborough's portrait of the Duchess of Devonshire.

Charles Thornton, (1820–81), owned the Old White Swan Inn in Swan Street and was the proprietor of the Varieties Music Hall (now called the Leeds City Varieties). In 1873 he built a block of shops and offices, Thornton's Buildings, where the Upper Headrow meets with Lands Lane. In 1875 Thornton sought permission to demolish the Old Talbot Inn on Briggate, to build a new arcade of shops on the site. The Talbot was not just any old pub; it was one of the oldest inns in Leeds and boasted frescoes on the walls of a room there. The inn was a venue for cockfighting, and in the seventeenth century it was where the circuit judge stayed while in Leeds.

26. University of Leeds Brotherton Library (1885), Parkinson Building

The Brotherton Library is a Grade II-listed Beaux-Arts building with art deco Fittings, completed in 1936 and named after Edward Brotherton, who bequeathed £100,000 as funding for the University of Leeds' first purpose-built library in 1927. In the beginning, while the university was still Leeds College, it stocked all of the university's books and manuscripts, except the books housed in the separate Medical Library and Clothworkers' Textile Library. Nowadays, it provides the home for the collections in arts, social sciences and law, and various special collections, archives and gallery.

The first library here dates from 1894 and was in the undercroft of College Hall, part of the Yorkshire College, originally founded as the Leeds School of Medicine in 1831. The college became part of the Victoria University in 1887. Fanny Passavant was the first librarian; she retired in 1919 when the library, bursting at the seams, contained 65,000 volumes. The façade of the Parkinson building is of Portland stone, but the exterior of the Brotherton Library is plain red brick. This is because access was to be through the Parkinson Building, so there was no need to have a Portland stone exterior when the library was obscured. However, lack of funding delayed the completion of the Parkinson so the Brotherton's bland exterior was visible for fourteen years.

There is absolutely nothing bland about the splendid interior: it is modelled on the old reading room at the British Museum – although, with a diameter of 160 feet, it is deliberately wider than the 140 feet of the British Museum Reading Room. Twenty columns of green Swedish marble, each comprising three 3-ton drums, support the coffered dome; the surrounding balcony has an ornate iron balustrade and an art deco electrolier hangs from the dome's centre.

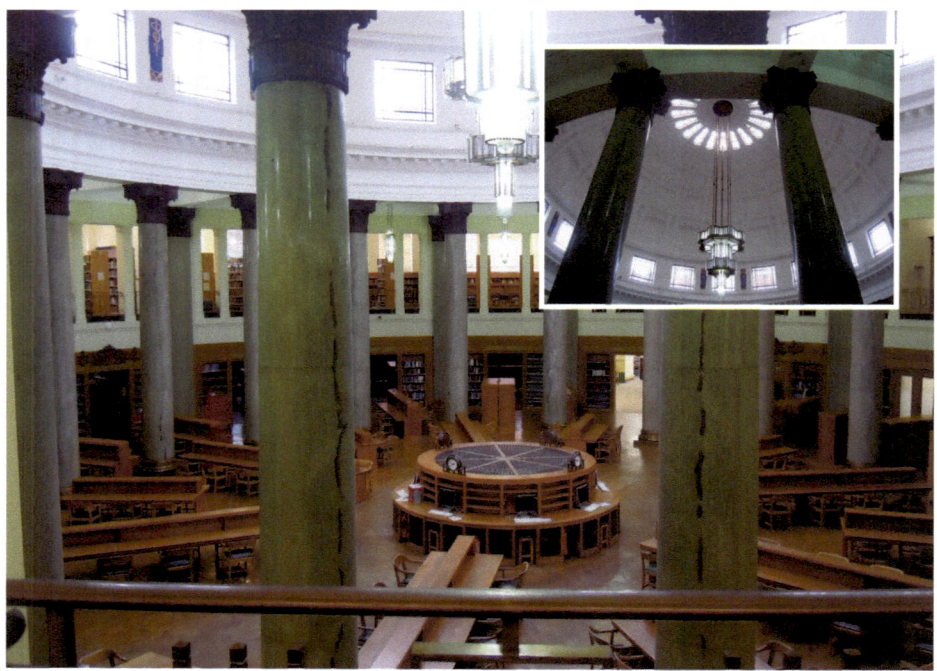

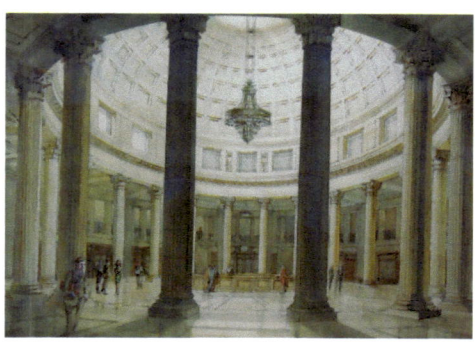

The Brotherton Library today, and soon after construction. Designed deliberately to surpass the size and beauty of the old Reading Room at the old British Library.

Treasures include locks of hair from the heads of Mozart and Beethoven, Shakespeare's First Folio – Mr *William Shakespeare's Comedies, Histories. & Tragedies*, Newton's *Philosophiæ Naturalis Principia Mathematica* (1687) and Oscar Wilde's 1883 manuscript *The Duchess of Padua*.

27. Leeds Art Gallery (1888), The Headrow

The gallery opened on 3 October 1888 as Leeds City Art Gallery. Leeds Art Gallery, as it is now called, has been described as 'Probably the best collection of twentieth-century British art outside London' (John Russell Taylor, *The Times*).

The twentieth-century exhibits are officially regarded as a collection 'of national importance'.

To prove that, it includes works by local artists such as Henry Moore, Barbara Hepworth, Atkinson Grimshaw, Jacob Kramer, as well as from a range of contemporary artists including Bridget Riley, Antony Gormley and Francis Bacon. Rodin also features.

Sir Henry Spencer Moore (1898–1986) studied at Leeds Art College in 1919. He became the first student of sculpture there when the college set up a sculpture studio especially for him. At the college, Moore met Barbara Hepworth who was to become a lifelong friend.

Other gems include paintings by Turner and Cotman. Atkinson Grimshaw is represented by numerous characteristically Victorian works. French art is represented by Derain and Sisley. Through the Henry Moore Foundation, the gallery has been able to amass a modern sculpture collection second only to that of the Tate in London. The gallery is linked by a bridge to the Henry Moore Institute dedicated to the study of sculpture. This came about in 1976 when it was decided to remodel and extend the gallery and name it after Henry Moore, who donated £2 million worth of his prize works to the complex, as well as his collection of maquettes. It reopened in 1982 as The Art Gallery and the Henry Moore Institute.

The new building restored the old public reading room, the lecture room and part of the old sculpture gallery. The original cast-iron columns in the reading room were retained, and the entrance and arcaded framework of the lecture theatre restored. A public house and a craft centre were built in the basement. A statue, *Reclining Woman 80*, by Henry Moore was situated outside the entrance.

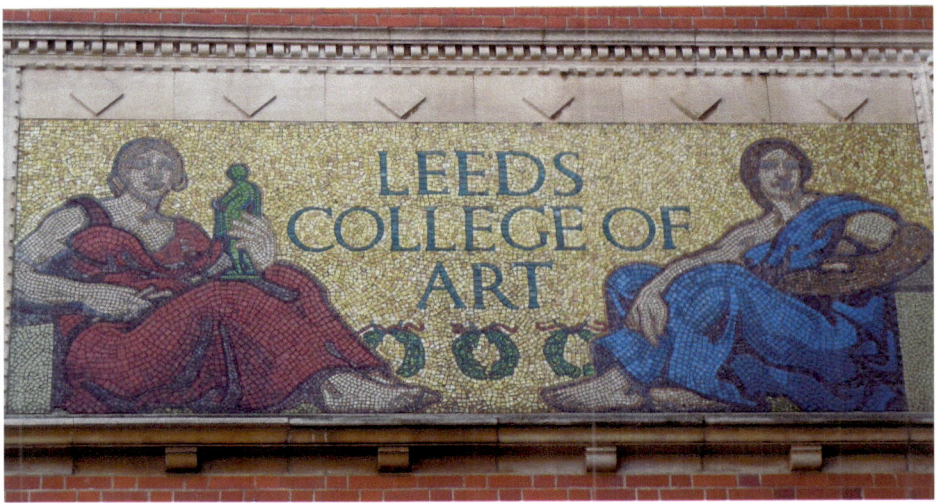

The superb mosaic at the old College of Art, concealed almost behind the City Museum, then the Mechanics' Institute.

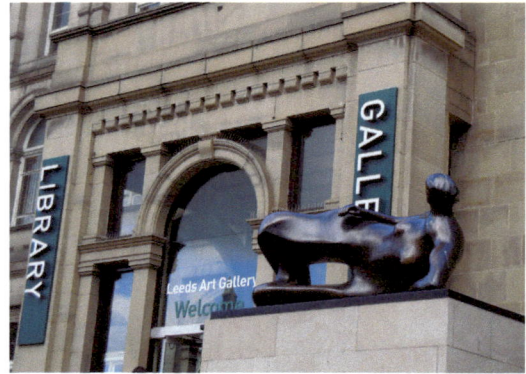

Reclining Woman '80.

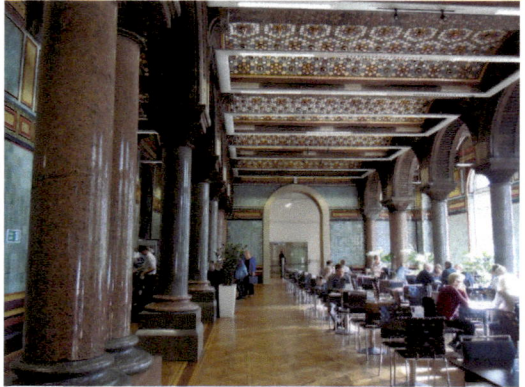

The magnificent Tile Hall, originally the Sculpture Room, now a café. Before it housed the sculpture it was the Reading Room from 1888 and housed the Commercial and Technical Library from 1955. The 2007 restoration has made the most of the colourful tiles and the beautiful parquet floor.

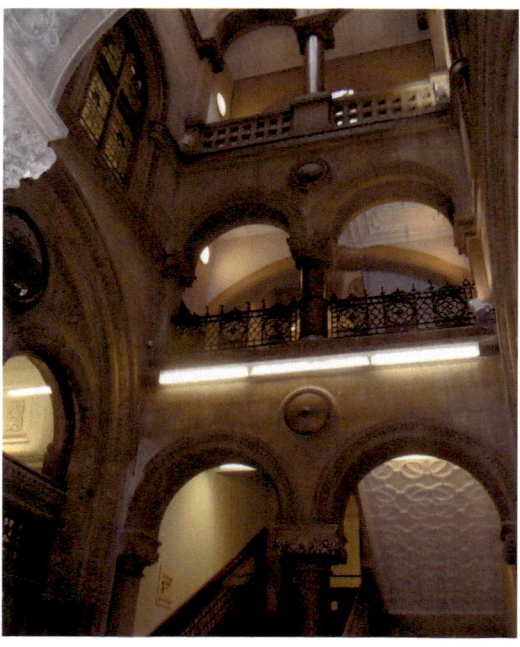

The equally magnificent main staircase.

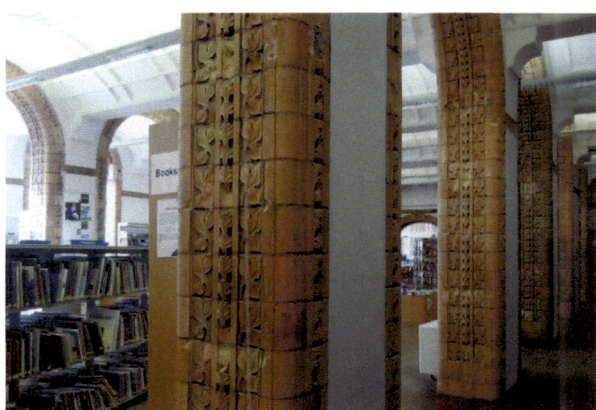

The art library with its stunning ornate arches.

In 1986 a new wing was built onto the back of the existing gallery. The Grade II-listed building underwent major renovation in 2007. This opened up the glorious Victorian tiled hall which now houses the café and bookshop and links the gallery and the library.

28. Queen's Arcade (1889), Victoria Quarter, off Briggate

Queen's Arcade was built on the site of the Rose and Crown Yard in 1889, and named to honour Queen Victoria's Golden Jubilee. The arcade is two storeys high, with a glass roof, with access to the second storey by a cast-iron curved balcony. The second storey housed shops, but it was originally where the shopkeepers lived. The floor of the balcony is an iron frame inset with glass pavement lights to allow light through to the shop fronts below.

When it opened the *Yorkshire Post* described it as 'light, bright and architecturally elegant, and is moreover, admirably designed from the business point of view'.

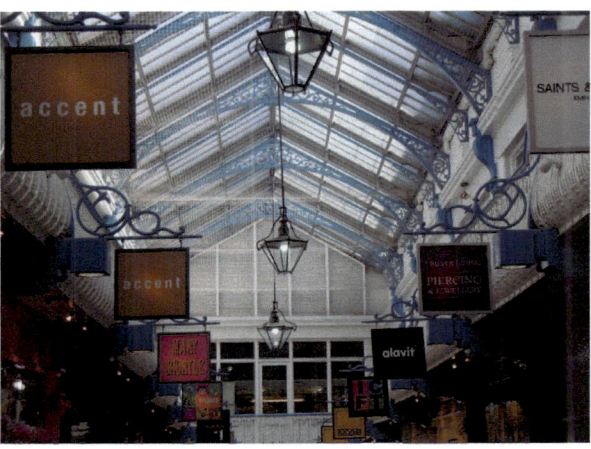

Queen's Arcade.

29. The Calls (c. 1890)

The Calls area along with nearby Clarence Dock were bustling docks on the Leeds and Liverpool Canal and the Aire and Calder Navigation during the Industrial Revolution and the early twentieth century. The first White Cloth Hall of 1711 moved here in 1776. Leeds Grammar School started its days here. The waterways teemed with barges, cranes and warehouses; they buzzed with forgers, malters, brewers, longshoremen and stone merchants. At Sparrow's Wharf a seven-storey warehouse dating from the early nineteenth century survives as a Grade II-listed building (No. 32 The Calls). It features fourteen first-floor openings and a tier of loading doors on each side of the building; the building has seen service as a corn merchants, clothing factory and wines and spirits merchants.

Four warehouses including Fletland Mills, now Grade II listed as Nos 40 and 42 The Calls, were converted to a hotel and restaurant, known as 42 The Calls in 1991, tastefully incorporating many of the original features and working mill machinery – 'oak beams, industrial girders and mill gears protrude from the ceiling'.

In its heyday, Fletland Mills spearheaded a revolution in the British milling industry and had a hand in the establishment of the Co-op. Disgusted at the routine adulteration of the local flour and the attendant profiteering, seven Leeds flax-mill workers established their own flour mill, which grew into the Leeds Co-operative society. It was the largest Co-op group in the country, even forming its own navy, which gave protection and brought down shipping costs. The hotel website (42thecalls.com) takes up the story:

> In 1887, after nearly sixty years in the milling trade, the Wright brothers acquired the underperforming eighteenth and nineteenth century Fletland Mills located at No. 42 The Calls. Bringing in new working practices and other elements of change, the company quickly turned around the fortunes of the mill, expanded it and produced record quantities of flour and corn meal for the district of Leeds. Ideally located on the River Aire, this industrial hub became a benchmark for millers across the county, and fast gained a reputation as one of the best suppliers in the UK.

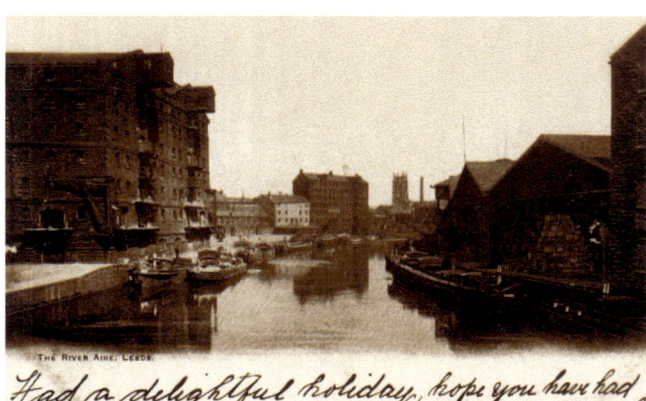

Warehouses lining the River Aire in 1908.

Nowadays, The Calls, Call Lane and Lower Briggate are Leeds' main gay district, with many pubs and bars. The most notable perhaps is The New Penny (formerly the Hope & Anchor), the UK's longest-running gay pub which opened in 1982. The Calls is also where the Leeds Pride post-parade street party is held.

30. Headingley (1891), Street Michael's Lane, Headingley

Today Headingley Stadium is a truly multi-sport stadium, being home to Yorkshire County Cricket Club, Leeds Rhinos rugby league team and Yorkshire Carnegie rugby union club.

It comprises two separate grounds: Headingley Carnegie Cricket Stadium and Headingley Carnegie Rugby Stadium, with one two-sided stand common to both. The ground is managed jointly by Yorkshire CCC and Leeds Rugby. The official name since 2006 has been the Headingley Carnegie Stadium due to sponsorship by Leeds Beckett University whose sports faculty is known as the Carnegie School of Sport Exercise and Physical Education.

The cricket ground, which opened in 1891, occupies the northern side of the complex and has been in service for Test matches since 1890. The first Test was England versus Australia in 1890; 2014 saw the first ever Test match at the venue between England and Sri Lanka. To date Headingley has hosted seventy-three Tests.

It was first floodlit in 2015 and has a seated capacity of 17,500; executive facilities and a new media centre opened in 2010. Apart from being home to Yorkshire County Cricket Club, Yorkshire Vikings Twenty20 cricket team also play their matches there. In 2006, Yorkshire CCC rebuilt the stand adjacent to the rugby ground, taking the capacity to 20,000. It also redeveloped the Winter Shed (North) stand creating a £12.5 million pavilion complex.

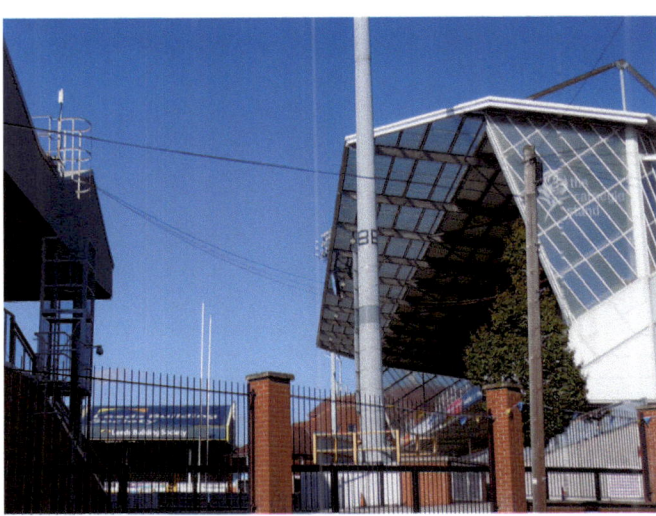

The Carnegie Stand at Headingley on a sunny day in October 2015.

The 21,000-capacity rugby ground consists of three stands and an open terrace at one end: one stand is an all-seater, one is standing and one mixed.

The first rugby league match was played at the stadium on 20 September 1890 when Leeds beat Manningham. In 1913, Leeds set the record for the highest ever score at Headingley when they beat Coventry 102-0: Fred Webster scored eight tries – every Leeds player scored a try that day.

31. The Grand Arcade (1898), Merrion Street

The Grand Arcade was built between Briggate and Vicar Lane in 1898 by the New Briggate Arcade Company Ltd. It takes its name from the Grand Theatre. The arcade is two storeys, with a glazed roof, but is somewhat less ornate than Thornton's and the Queen's Arcade.

In 1920 one avenue of shops was closed to make way for the Tower cinema. Like Thornton's it has an impressive clock: the dial is mounted between two knights in armour who strike the quarter hours. On the hour, a door opens to allow five figures to emerge on a revolving stage. These figures exemplify Great Britain and her empire and include a British Grenadier Guardsman, a Scotsman, an Irishman, a Canadian, and an Indian; they soon disappear into a door to the right to make way for a cockerel which nods its head, flaps wings and crows.

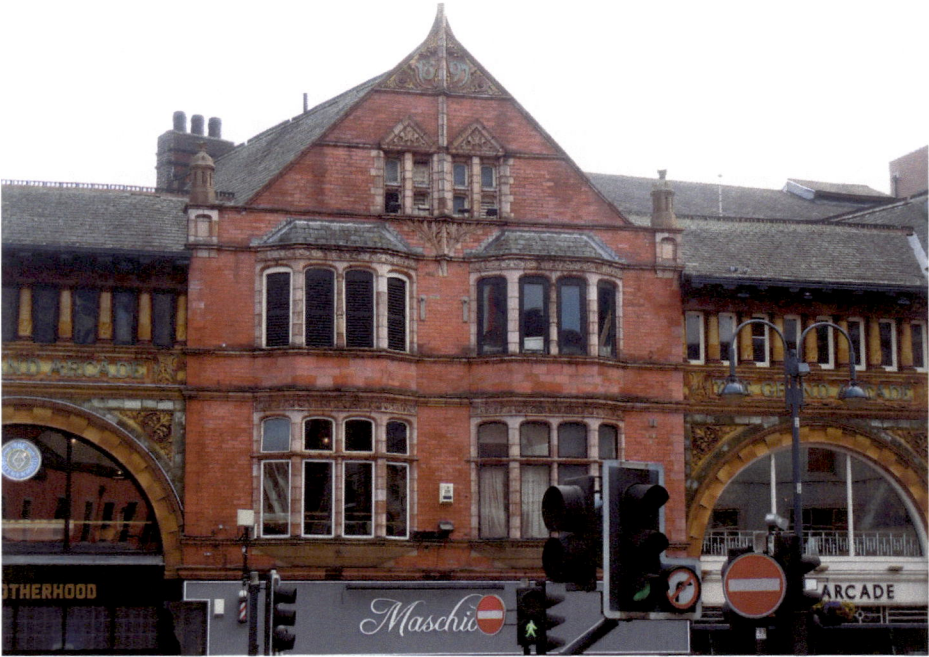

The Grand Arcade and its ornate arches.

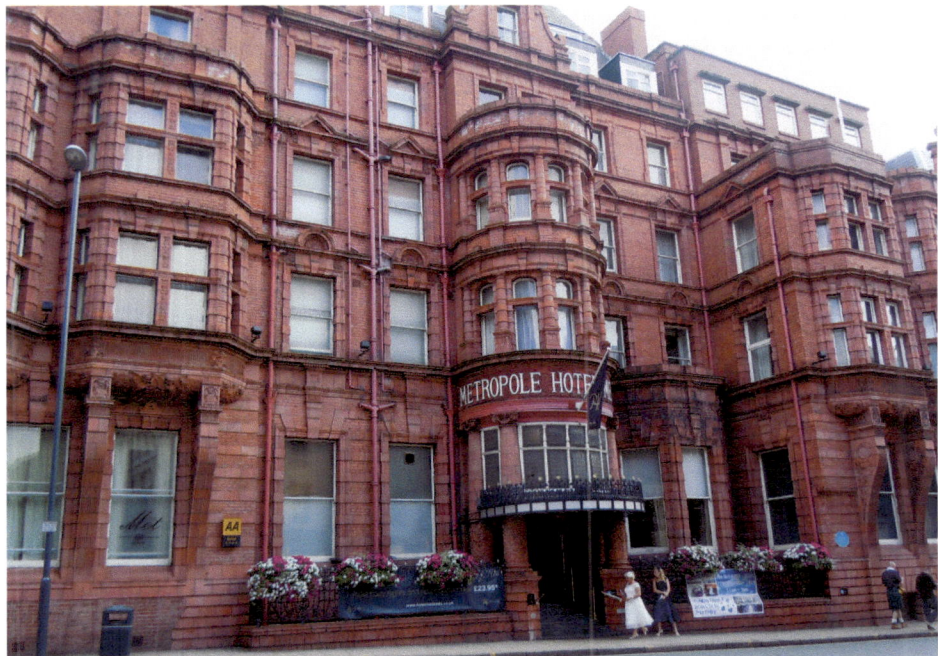

The Metropole with wedding guests and a Scotsman in kilt on his way to the Rugby World Cup match versus the USA on 26 September 2015. Scotland won 39-16.

32. The Met Hotel (1898), King Street

A Grade II-listed building on King Street completed in 1898 as the 120-room Hotel Metropole; it was the recipient of a £6 million renovation in 2005.

The standout features of the hotel are its rare and marvellous Victorian terracotta façade and the cupola on the roof which was taken from the demolished fourth White Cloth Hall, built in 1868 on the same site.

33. County Arcade and Cross Arcade (1903), Victoria Quarter, off Briggate

County Arcade and Cross Arcade were built between 1898 and 1903 on the site of the White Horse Yard creating a new street on each side of the arcade: Wood Street became Queen Victoria Street, and Cheapside became King Edward Street on the site of the New Shambles and the fish market.

These ornate arcades were designed by Frank Matcham and were two storeys high with shops confined to the ground level. There are pink marble columns between the mahogany shop fronts, and there is elaborate Burmantofts faience work above the cast-iron balustrades. The vaulted ceiling is glass with three domes displaying mosaic figures representing liberty, commerce, labour and art.

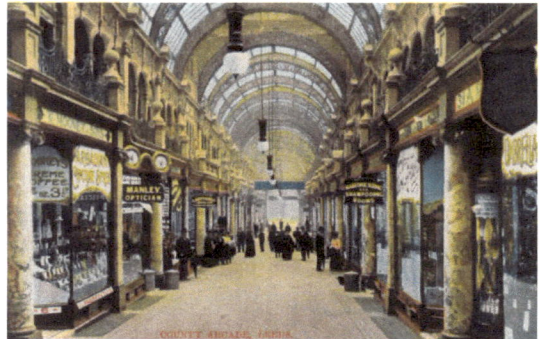

County Arcade in the 1910s, called so because the original market cross was on this site. One of the places in the arcade around 1906 was the 1903 Ceylon Café, later a J. Lyons House. It boasted an ornate ceiling, balcony and pillars with a large fountain (with no water) in the centre. Other J. Lyons cafés opened in Bond Street in 1908 and the Grand Arcade in 1910.

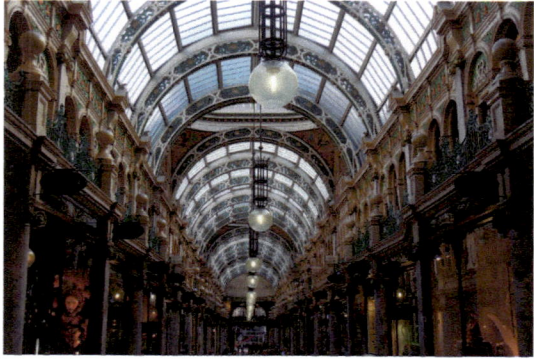

A similar view in 2015.

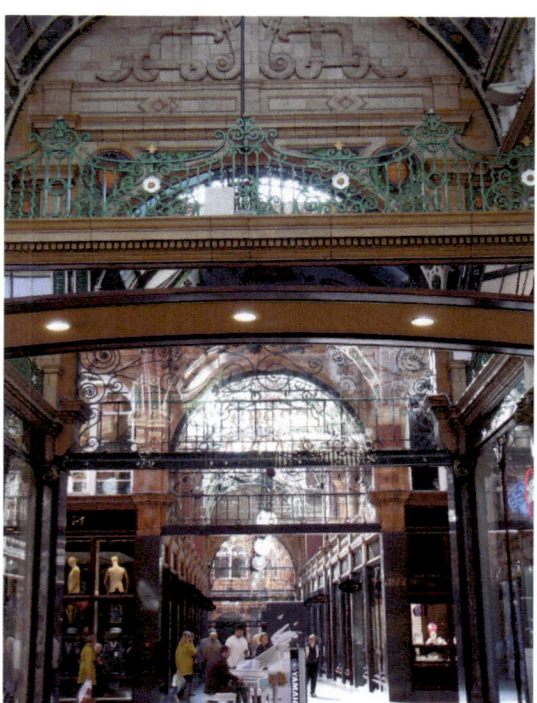

Cross Arcade in 2015. Cross Arcade runs between King Edward Street and what was Queen Victoria Street. This is now all part of the Victoria Quarter refurbished in 1989 and 1990. The rear entrance to Harvey Nichols Department store (Nos 107–111 Briggate) is on the left side of the Cross Arcade. This was formerly an entrance to the Empire Arcade, which ran between Briggate and the Cross Arcade. Before that it was the site of the Empire Theatre which was demolished in 1962.

The Cross Arcade contained the rear entrance to the Empire Arcade. The Empire Arcade opened in 1964 after the demolition of the Empire Theatre in 1962 to be replaced by Harvey Nichols. The main entrance to the Empire Arcade was on Briggate.

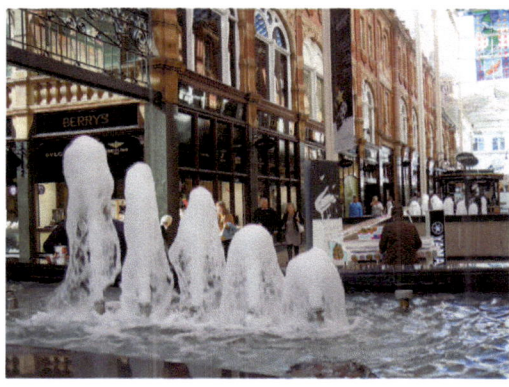

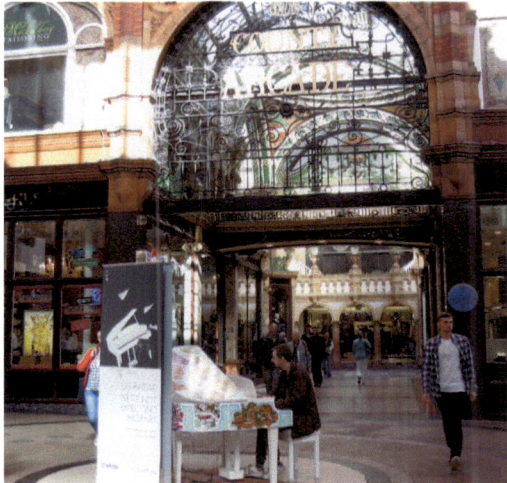

Marks & Spencer had their first 'Original Penny Bazaar' outside the original market location here in Cross Arcade, where it operated from 1904. In 1909, a new shop opened at No. 76 Briggate, which was extended to Queen's Arcade in 1926.

34. Barnbow Munitions Factory (1914), Cross Gates

Barnbow was a First World War munitions factory located between Cross Gates and Garforth, officially known as National Filling Factory No. 1. Sadly, Barnbow is best known for the massive explosion which killed thirty-five of the women workers in 1916.

When war was declared, shells were being filled and armed at Leeds Forge Co., Armley, which by August 1915 was filling 10,000 shells every week. This however, was insufficient to meet demand so a committee, chaired by Joseph Watson, the Leeds soap manufacturer, was set up to build a new munitions factory.

Railway tracks were laid running into the factory complex to carry materials in and finished goods out. Platforms over 800 feet (240 m) long were added to the nearby railway station to help transport workers to and from work at the site; power lines were erected to bring power and a water main was laid to deliver 200,000 gallons of water per day. Shell filling work began in December 1915.

One third of the staff was from Leeds while others commuted from York, Castleford, Wakefield, and Harrogate; by October 1916 the workforce exceeded 16,000 people, 93 per cent of whom were women and girls – the Barnbow Lasses. Earnings averaged £3 per week, though bonuses allowed women handling the explosives to take home up to £12 per week. Thirty-eight trains per day – Barnbow Specials – carried the workers to and from work.

Working conditions were nothing short of hell: workers who handled the explosives stripped to their underwear, and wore smocks, caps, rubber gloves and rubber-soled shoes to avoid sparks. Cigarettes and matches were obviously banned, as were combs and hairpins to prevent static electricity. There were no holidays; shifts were eight hours long. Workers were allowed to drink as much barley water and milk as they liked and, to help with the milk, Barnbow had its own farm, with a herd of 120 cows producing 300 gallons of milk per day. Working with Cordite turned the skin yellow and the only antidote was milk. Because of the yellowness of the women's skin, the women were called the Barnbow Canaries.

On Tuesday 5 December 1916, 170 women and girls had just started their night shift:

> 4 ½ inch shells were being filled, fused, and packed in Room 42. At 10:27 p.m. there was a massive explosion which killed thirty-five women outright, maimed and injured many more. Many of the dead were only identifiable by the identity disks. Production was interrupted only for a short time, and once the bodies were recovered, other girls immediately volunteered to work in Room 42.

None of this was made public until 1924; at the time death notices appeared in the *Yorkshire Evening Post*, simply stating cause of death as 'killed by accident'. There were two further explosions at the factory, the first in March 1917 killing

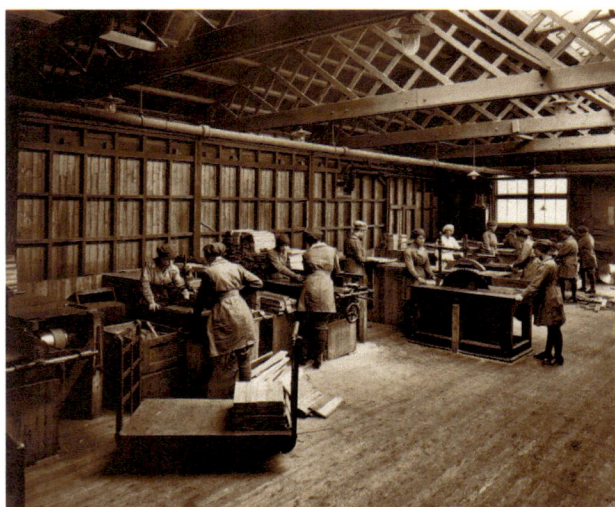

Barnbow girls making box lids for cartridge packing cases out of empty propellant boxes. They are using circular saws (without guards, of course) to cut the wood to size to make the box lids. Live material from waste material.

two girl workers, the other in May 1918 killing three men. Barnbow was Britain's premier shell factory between 1914 and 1918. By 11 November 1918, a total of 566,000 tons of ammunition had been shipped to the various fronts.

Apart from setting up the dignified memorial, in 2012 the people of Leeds named a number of parks, buildings and streets in memory of the Barnbow Lasses. The names of those who died are listed in the roll of honour in Colton Methodist church and in York Minster.

35. Hyde Park Picture House (1914), Brudnell Road

This marvellous-looking Grade II-listed picture house started life in 1908 as a hotel and in November 1914 was converted into the cinema, which still has its nine gas lights, the decorated Edwardian balcony and the original organ and piano. It is one of the oldest and one the few surviving picture palaces in the UK and is among the finest examples of Edwardian architecture in Leeds. With its 280-seater auditorium it retains its two 35mm film projectors which are still regularly used, especially during Leeds International Film Festival, during which the cinema serves as a main venue. The ornate lamp outside the entrance is also Grade II listed but no longer gas-powered.

The 1914 opening was promoted by an advertisement in the *Yorkshire Evening Post* which, amid all the war news, heralded the new picture house as 'the cosiest in Leeds'. Apart from patriotic films, the picture house also showed newsreels of the war to the people of Leeds, anxious to learn about the 6,000 men from Leeds who had enlisted and reliant on the picture house news because many of them could not read the newspapers or afford a wireless.

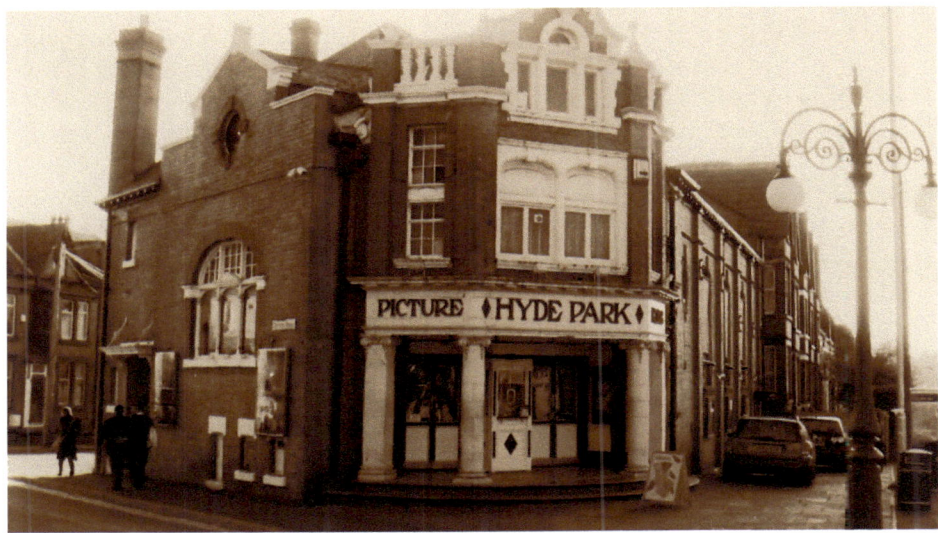

Hyde Park Picture House then.

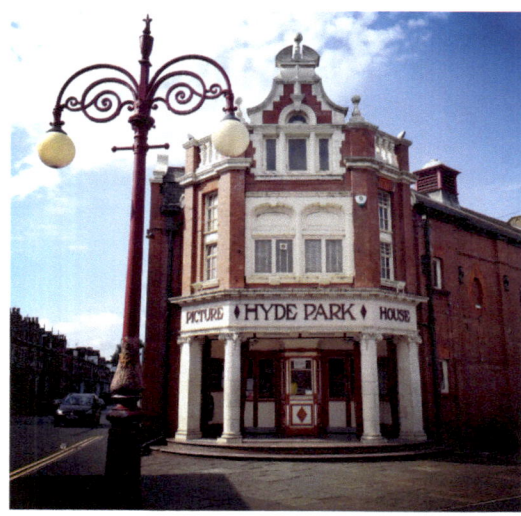

Hyde Park Picture House now.

36. Elland Road (1919)

Elland Road has been the home of Leeds United AFC since the club was founded in 1919; previously the ground was occupied by Leeds City FC and Holbeck Rugby Club. Bentley's Brewery owned it under the name of the Old Peacock Ground, after the nearby pub – hence the club's nickname the Peacocks. Holbeck Rugby Club moved in from Holbeck Recreation Ground after purchasing the Old Peacock Ground from Bentley's for £1,100.

The club built a new stand for the 1898/99 season and the ground became known as Elland Road. In the 1902/03 season the football team Leeds Woodville of the Leeds League shared the ground with Holbeck RLFC; they went under in 1904 and the ground was put up for sale. At a meeting at the Griffin Hotel in Boar Lane a new football club, Leeds City, was formed who rented Elland Road. City built a 5,000-seater covered stand on the west side. Attendances were on the up with the high point being the 22,500 who squashed into the stadium for a local derby with Bradford City in 1904, raking in £487 of gate money. In 1906 the club built a 4,000-seater grandstand using over half a mile of steel and comprising a training track that ran the length of the stand, dressing and officials' rooms and a garage. Drainage work was carried to improve drainage on the pitch. During the First World War the ground was used for drill and shooting practice. However, illegal payments made to players during the war led to expulsion from the Football League after only eight games and some local businessmen toyed with the idea of digging up the clay deposits under the pitch and converting the ground into a brickyard. Yorkshire Amateurs were installed as the tenants, and in 1920 sold Elland Road to the newly formed Leeds United for the knock-down price of £250. Leeds City are the only club to be expelled from the League mid-season, and the only club to be invited to leave the League due to financial irregularities.

In 1920 Leeds United were elected to the Second Division of the Football League, gaining promotion as Champions in 1924, only to be relegated in 1927. The 1920s were a time of much development: the South Stand terrace was overlaid with a wooden barrel-shaped roof and was known as the Scratching Shed; Lowfields Stand was built on the east side. The terrace behind the goal at the north end was known as the Spion Kop, or Kop, from the famous hill in South Africa where 322 British soldiers lost their lives in January 1900, during the Second Boer War. On 27 December 1932, 56,796 spectators watched Leeds United play the eventual champions, Arsenal. The stadium hosted the all Leeds Rugby Football League Championship Final between Leeds and Hunslet in 1938: a crowd of 54,112 saw Hunslet win the title. The ground was requisitioned by the War Office during the Second World War.

Floodlights were first switched on in November 1953 for a match against Hibernian. This attracted 31,500 spectators who saw two goals each from legends John Charles and manager Raich Carter in a 4-1 victory. On Tuesday 18 September 1956, a fire tore through the West Stand destroying offices, kit, club records, physiotherapy equipment, dressing rooms, directors' rooms, the press box and the generators for the floodlighting system. Insurance cover was inadequate so the directors launched an appeal to build a new stand with help from Leeds City Council. The appeal raised £60,000 and the £180,000 West Stand was opened in time for the start of the following season with 4,000 seats rising behind an area which held 6,000 standing spectators.

Don Revie's reign as manager in the 1960s saw major successful developments at the ground both on and off the pitch. On 15 March 1967, in a fifth round FA Cup replay against Sunderland, a new attendance record of 57,892 was set; in 1968 the Spion Kop terracing was replaced by a new stand known as the Gelderd End. The 60 feet (18 m) of land left behind the goal was turfed and the pitch moved 30 feet (9.1 m) to the north.

In 1970 the West Stand was joined to the Kop with a corner stand, known as the North-West corner while another linked the Lowfields Stand and the Kop. In 1974 Leeds won the title for the second time and the Scratching Shed was replaced by the South Stand, comprising an all-standing paddock for 4,000 fans, and sixteen executive boxes, above which was an all-seater 3,500 capacity stand. That same year the floodlights were replaced by Europe's tallest floodlights, at a height of 260 feet (79 m).

A banqueting suite at the back of the West Stand, with a conference centre, was opened in 1992. The same year the Lowfields was replaced by a new 17,000-seater two-tier East Stand with twenty-five executive boxes, 10,000 seats in the lower tier, part of which was the family section, and a further 7,000 seats in the upper tier. At the time the East Stand was then the biggest cantilever stand in the world. In 1994 Elland Road became an all-seater stadium, with almost 7,000 seats filling the Kop after the *Taylor Report*. The Gelderd End was renamed the Don Revie Stand.

The pitch measures 105 m long by 68 m wide, with an under-soil heating system consisting of 59 miles of piping. The club has its own water supply from wells

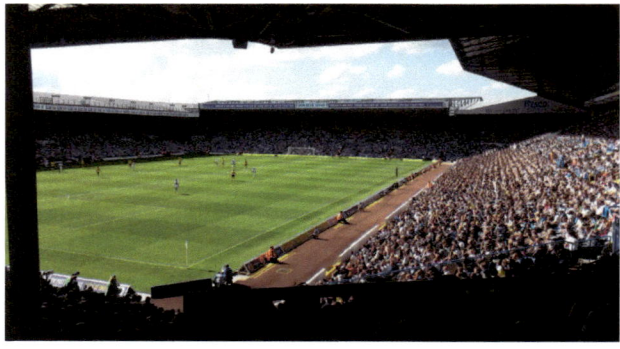

Capacity crowd at Elland Road from the south-east corner.

sunk beneath the West and North Stands and a pumping system under the South Stand. However, the first time it was used, the pitch turned black as the water was too cold.

Today the capacity is 37,914. Rugby League returned to the ground when Hunslet Hawks played there for several seasons in the mid-1980s.

37. Burton's (1932), Hudson Road

What was to become Burton's was opened on 17 September 1932 as a Lewis's department store – a store with a greater variety of goods than any other in Leeds. Footfall on that opening day was over 100,000 people.

'Ask Me' girls were busy helping people navigate the 157 different departments which sold everything from furniture to food. New features included the escalators – the first to be installed in Leeds. The only item to run out that day were lobsters at 9*d* each. A major refurbishment was completed in 2009 with individual retail units let to the usual high street suspects.

Burton's was founded by Montague Burton in Chesterfield in 1904 under the name of The Cross-Tailoring Co. Burton himself was originally called Meshe David Osinsky, a Russian-Jewish immigrant. He arrived in England from Russia aged fifteen working as a peddler, and three years later borrowed £100 from a relative to open The Cross-Tailoring Co. Records show that the first purchase of ready-made suits was on 8 June 1905, from Zimmerman Bros, wholesale clothiers of Leeds. The growing business moved to Elmwood Mills, Camp Road, in Leeds, but by 1914 it had outgrown these premises and transferred to Concord Mills, Concord Street, in the Leylands.

By 1914 the number of Burton shops increased to fourteen and their made-to-measure service was well on the way to becoming the largest in the world. The First World War saw production make the transition from suits to uniforms, clothing nearly 25 per cent of the armed forces. Retail sales grew from £52,000 in 1915 to £140,000 in 1917.

From 1921 Burton developed the factory in Hudson Road into the biggest clothing factory in the world, employing 1,000 men and 9,000 women workers

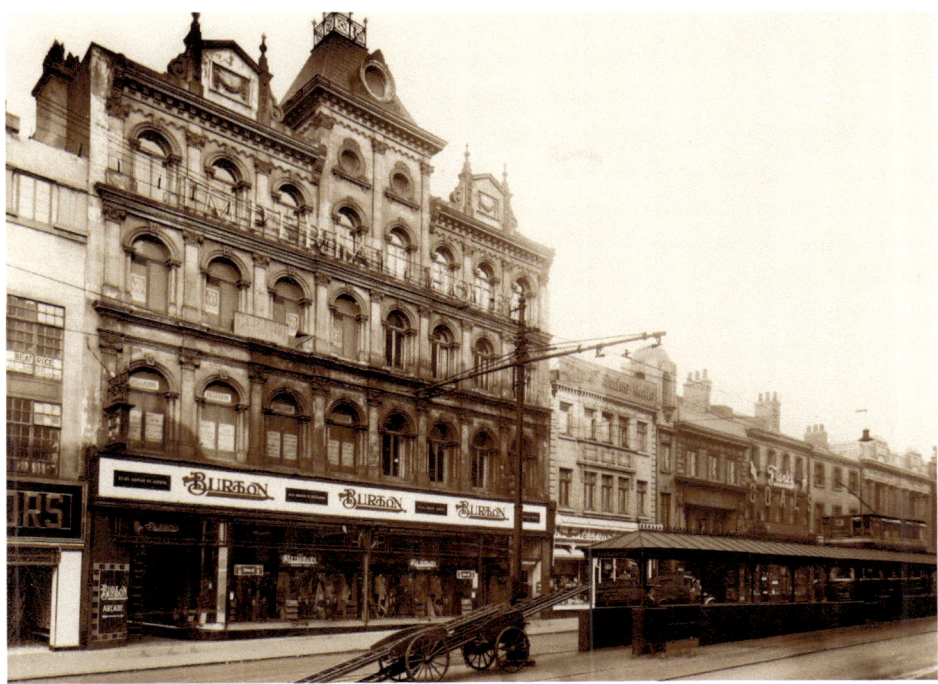

Burton's grand old shop and arcade beneath the Imperial Hotel on Briggate. The arcade was previously known as the George and Dragon Yard after the pub there. The hotel was famous for Nelson's billiard hall. In 1961 the entire building was demolished so that Burton's could build a new store on the site. The J. Lyons café next door advertises Lyons Swiss Rolls from a sign on top of the building. Note the tram stops and two handcarts with ladders. (Courtesy of Leodis; © Leeds Library & Information Services)

and producing over 30,000 suits a week – Leeds' biggest employer in the city. Men would begin their careers at fourteen as barrow boys then take apprenticeships as tailors and cutters. There were huge workrooms of women machinists with whole families working on the same production line. The factory was described as 'a town itself'. Like the Rowntrees before him in York, Burton was an enlightened employer: Hudson Road had the largest canteen in the world and workers benefitted from a (pre-welfare state) health and pension scheme. There were dentists, optometrists and ophthalmologists (to treat eye strain brought on by close needlework), chiropodists and sunray treatment – all to maintain a healthy and productive workforce.

By the time Burton's was first listed on the London Stock Exchange in 1929 it had 400 stores, factories and mills. The goal was to provide men with good quality suits at the cost of a week's wages (a 'five guinea suit for fifty-five shillings'). By the 1930s the self-styled 'tailor of taste' had built a chain of 500 shops that were instantly recognisable on British high streets, with their bold art deco motifs, including stylised elephants' heads, faience panels, bronzed metal and polished granite.

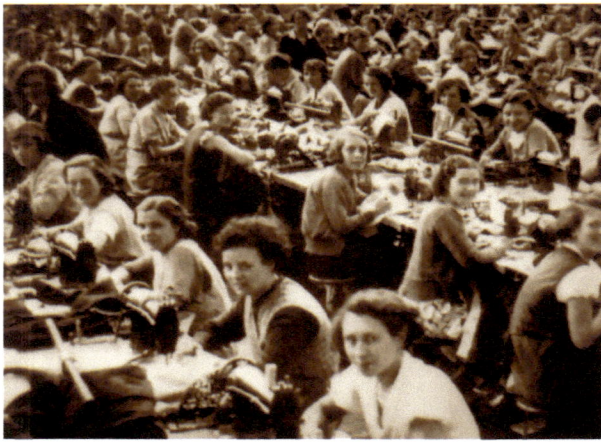

Busy at work in the Burton's factory in Hudson Road, Harehills.

At the end of the Second World War, Montague Burton was one of the chief suppliers of demob suits, comprising jacket, trousers, waistcoat, shirt and underwear. This is the derivation of the phrase 'the full Monty'. By the end of the war, Burton was probably clothing around 20 per cent of British men. Legend has it that there was an RAF office over a Burton's shop somewhere where servicemen would sit exams. Failing candidates were said to have 'Gone for a Burton'.

When Burton died in 1952 the company was the largest multiple tailor in the world with 616 stores. Burton suited the England World Cup winners in 1966. He is commemorated in the Montague Burton Residences, student flats at the University of Leeds, the Montague Burton Professorship of International Relations at the University of Oxford and the Montague Burton Professorship of International Relations at London School of Economics. The Arcadia Group, of which Burton is part of, still uses the Leeds factory as offices and for warehousing.

38. Leeds Civic Hall (1933), Millennium Square

Leeds Civic Hall is the home of Leeds City Council in Millennium Square. It assumed the municipal responsibilities and functions from Leeds Town Hall in order to contain all the different council departments under one roof. Its construction took place during the Depression and was a fine example of a Keynesian job creation scheme, giving good, useful work to men who otherwise would have languished on the dole. It includes the lord mayor's room, council chambers and a banqueting hall.

The prestigious and influential Leeds Philosophical and Literary Society, founded in 1819, moved here from Park Row after its building was damaged in the Second World War. Among the founding fathers – a truly visionary cross-section of Leeds society – were Edward Baines, proprietor of the *Leeds Mercury* and MP, Benjamin Gott, father of the Yorkshire Woollen industry, Charles Thackray, town surgeon, and John Marshall, flax spinner. The society founded a museum in its own premises in Park Row which became the basis of today's City Museum in 1920. In 1936 the society donated its library and archive to the Brotherton Library of the University of Leeds.

The architect was George Corson, a descendent of the Italian architect Corsini, who in the thirteenth century was responsible for Sweetheart Abbey at Dumfries. Corson also designed Tetley's brewery as well as many other Leeds buildings. In 1877 it was decided to incorporate the Central Library which then was in the old infirmary on Infirmary Street. The building is in the Italianate style: the façade is particularly ornate.

The *British Architect* said of it: 'the eye roamed over a profusion of graceful arcades and stately pillars, whose effect is very striking, reminding one more of a Venetian palace than a Leeds corporate building'. Most of the original interior decoration survives, and the ornate staircase, carved animals, intricate carvings, and coloured tiles can still be seen.

The Municipal Buildings were opened with great pomp on 17 April 1884. That evening the mayor gave a banquet in the opulent Victoria Hall attended by the Home Secretary, Sir William Harcourt. The following evening, the mayor entertained over 1,000 poor people over the age of sixty in the Victoria Hall.

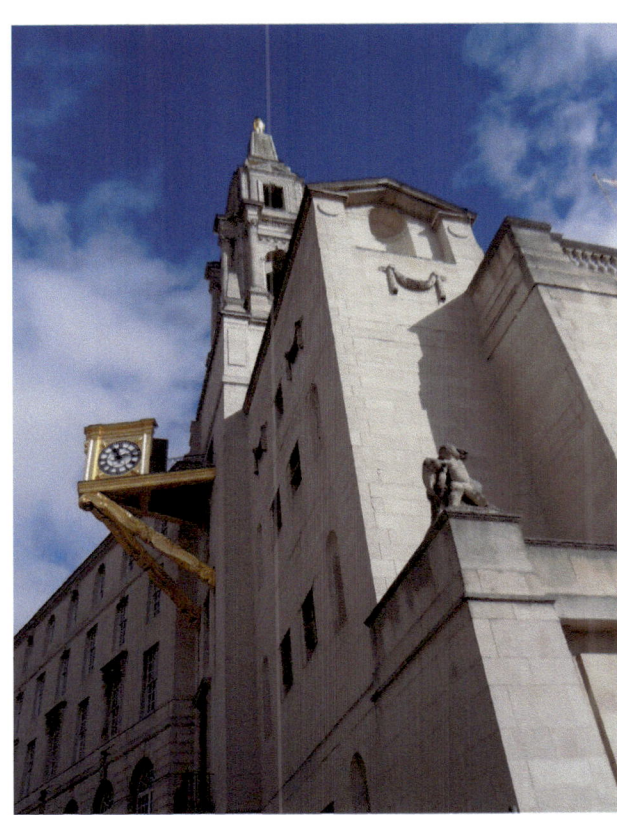

The magnificent clock on the 1933 Civic Hall with its four turtles. You can just see one of the two bronze owls (symbolic of Leeds) perched on one of the 170-foot towers – the birds are gilt surfaced, measuring 7 feet 6 inches and weighing half a ton.

39. The Warehouse (1979), Somers Street

The influential, groundbreaking Leeds Warehouse opened in 1979, even before Manchester's Hacienda. The Warehouse ushered in a new music-club culture and became the place for music and clubbing in the north of England.

Over the years here have been numerous magnificent, unforgettable sets – from Frankie Goes to Hollywood to Sugar Hill Gang, Oasis to The Stone Roses, Sasha, Greg Wilson, LFO and Mike Pickering. In May 2010 the club was sold, overhauled and refurbished to its former glory, restoring it as one of the cutting-edge venues in the history of house music and of contemporary music in general.

The Leeds Warehouse website gives us the facts:

> Of course, high on the agenda for the new owners has been the technology behind the light and sound systems to provide a venue that is simply untouchable in Leeds. Brand new Funktion One Dance Stacks tower above the dancefloor as well mind-blowing lighting rigs, colour lasers and CO_2 jets. Elsewhere, the venue has been remodelled throughout with a new layout, new chill-out areas, state of the art DJ equipment, new dance levels, new bars, new toilets and new air conditioning. Upstairs in the Loft the walls have been blasted back to expose the brick and huge wooden beams. Fireplaces and sash windows have been revealed to create a sumptuous second room overlooking The Warehouse. A new third room has been created by knocking through the main room into The Garage.

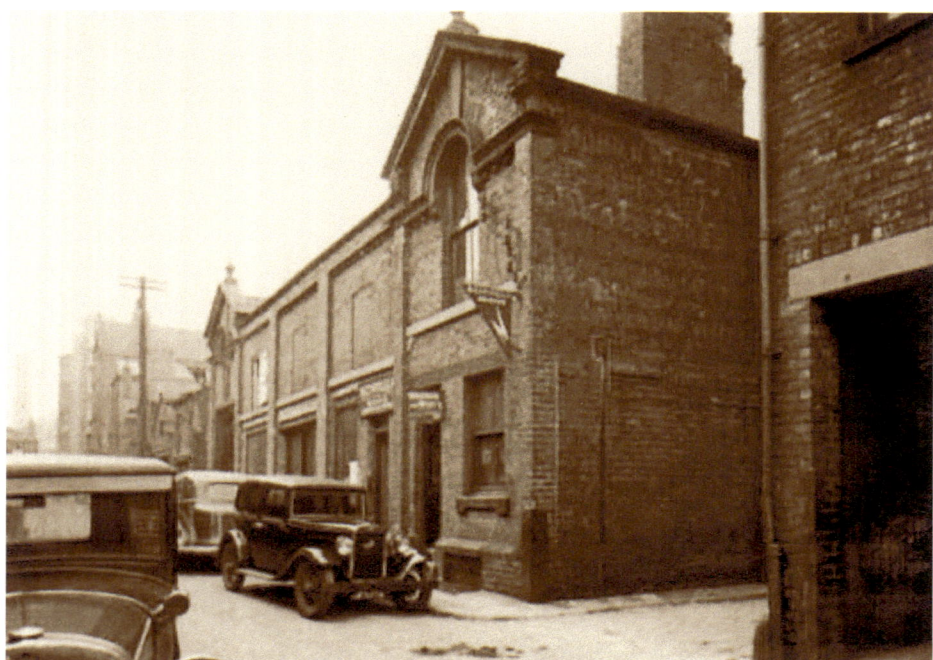

An early shot of what was to become the Wellington Building.

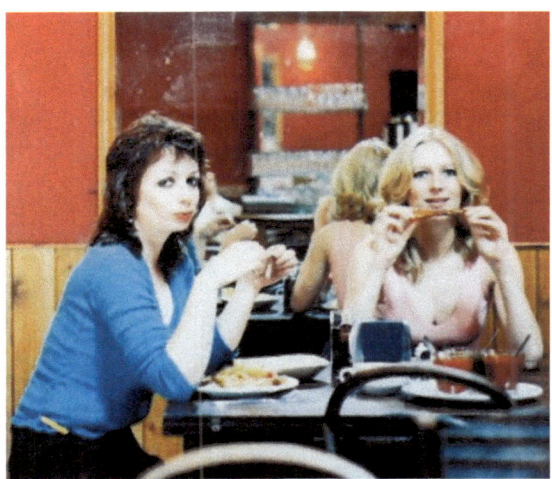

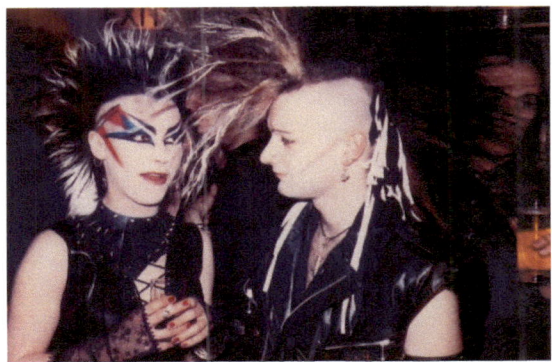

Life and varying fashions in the club.

40. West Yorkshire Playhouse (1990), Quarry Hill

The original Leeds Playhouse was a repertory theatre operating from a Portakabin. It then moved into the university sports hall on Calverley Street. During the 1970s the Leeds Theatre Trust began looking for a site for a permanent theatre. Two options were the old Gaumont Cinema (previously the Coliseum Theatre in Cookridge Street), and the Grand Theatre, to form part of a joint Grand/Playhouse theatre.

In the face of closure threats in 1984, Leeds City Council offered the Playhouse a new home on Quarry Hill, previously the site of the Quarry Hill flats, and £5.4 million funding. West Yorkshire County Council added a grant of £4 million towards the new theatre. Their beneficence was rewarded in the renaming of the Playhouse as the West Yorkshire Playhouse.

Donald Sinden turned the first sod in November 1987. The foundation stone was laid in March 1989 by Dame Judi Dench, and the topping out ceremony was performed by Albert Finney. Diana Rigg opened the theatre on 8 March 1990; Jude Kelly was appointed Artistic Director.

The new playhouse was Britain's largest new purpose-built theatre in fifteen years. It has two auditoria: the 750-seat Quarry theatre and the smaller 350-seat Courthouse Theatre.

41. Quarry House (1993), Quarry Hill

Quarry House was built on the site of the former Quarry Hill Flats at Quarry Hill. It houses the regional offices of the Department of Health and the Department for Work and Pensions. This powerful-looking building has earned itself the nicknames The Kremlin (photography is verboten), and the Ministry of Truth, after Orwell's *1984*.

It cost £55 million and keeps over 2,000 civil servants busy. When they are not so busy they can partake of the facilities at the Forum leisure centre: swimming pool, a sports hall, squash courts, and a fitness room 'fully equipped with the latest Polaris cardio-vascular, static-resistant and free-weight equipment', where civil servants can work out while watching TV. However, it is by no means cheap and costs employees £300 per year. The Woodpecker pub however, serves (tax payer) subsidised beer. Over £500,000 was spent on 'decorating' the building, under a government scheme requiring that 1 per cent of the cost of their new buildings be spent on art. Sadly, the people of Leeds do not see or cannot enjoy any of this.

Quarry House replaced Quarry Hill which, between 1938 and 1978, was, at the time, the biggest social-housing complex in the United Kingdom. Its design owed much to such modernist developments as the Karl-Marx-Hof in Vienna, and La Cité de la Muette in Paris. The homes at Quarry Hill could boast modern housing features such as solid fuel ranges, electric lighting, a state-of-the-art (but inefficient) refuse Garchey disposal system and communal facilities.

The original, grandiose plan was for 800 flats, but the height of the complex was increased to seven or eight storeys, and the number of flats to 938. In addition,

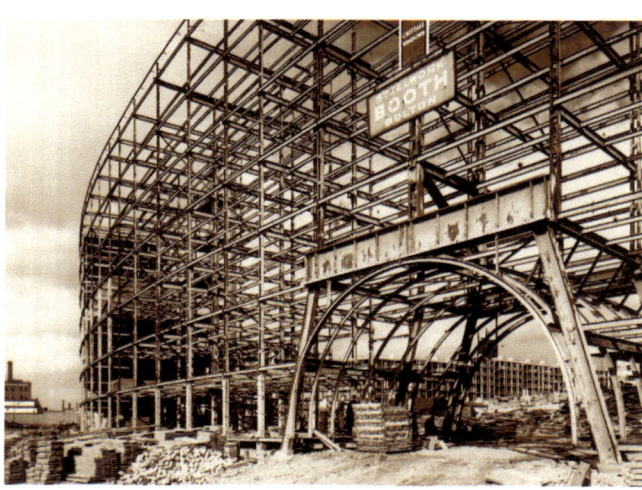

Quarry Hill under construction. (Courtesy of Leodis, © Leeds Library & Information Services)

there was a community hall with seating for 520 people including a stage and dressing rooms (never built), twenty shops (few opened), indoor and outdoor swimming pools, a paddling pool, courtyards and gardens. There was to be an estate nursery, playgrounds, lawns and recreation areas, a communal laundry with dryers (drying of clothes on the balconies was prohibited; all washing and drying was to be done here), and, to end it all, an estate mortuary. The swimming pools were replaced by tennis courts and a bowling green, but these too were never built. Eighty-eight two-person passenger lifts were fitted.

The flats themselves comprised a living room, scullery and bathroom and between one and five bedrooms. Each had a balcony with a coal hole and a window box. China cupboards, ventilated larder and airing cupboards were fitted as standard and all flats had electric lighting.

The living room had a gas point for a poker. A baking oven in the scullery was connected to an open coke grate in the living room. The master bedroom had a fitted wardrobe, and a coke grate with a gas point; there was an electric point for a fire and a corner hanging bracket in the second bedroom. There was a bath with a space-saving basin fitted over the end, and a WC. All flats had a point for radio and were palatial compared to a back to back with its outside toilet.

The revolutionary system used in construction was the Mopin System which deployed a light steel frame, encased in pre-cast-concrete units, which were then filled with concrete. All the floors, walls and ceilings were constructed from prefabricated concrete blocks on the site. The building was erected in stages, so did not need scaffolding. There was no brickwork or plastering, so no need for a skilled labour force. All this added up to significant savings in materials, time and labour costs, which made the scheme very economical.

The first group of flats opened in 1938 while building continued until 1941; however, the estate was never completed, and some of the flats were never lived in. Socially and architecturally all was not well and the Quarry Hill flats were demolished in 1978. The irony of it all was that Quarry Hill was intended to be the solution to the extensive social, environmental and health problems associated with the slums it replaced.

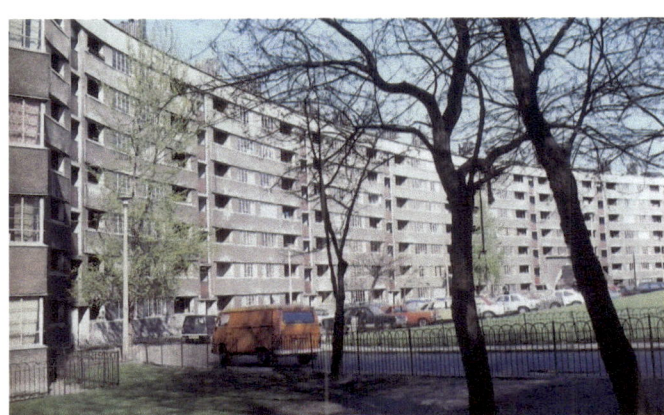

The ill-fated Quarry Hill in the '60s.

In 1914 Leeds, then the fifth largest city in England, had 78,000 back-to-backs. Back-to-back housing construction was made illegal in 1909 but a loophole in the law meant that new back-to-backs were still being built in Leeds during the 1930s. Something had to be done to clear the slums and eradicate the insanitary conditions they bred: one of those things that was done was the Quarry Hill project. By 1914, half the slum dwellings in the Quarry Hill area had been bulldozed.

Some milestones in the chequered history of Quarry Hill:

In the seventeenth century Quarry Hill, then outside the city limits, was home to plague cabins – a kind of concentration camp for the poor struck down with the plague. Isolation meant limited infection of other citizens.

Georgian Quarry Hill was a fashionable spa area where people came to take the waters. One of a number of Leeds spas – Quarry Hill – was linked with Sheepscar Beck and included the sulphuric waters of Spaw Well, Lady Well and St Peter's Well. St Peter's waters were efficacious against rheumatism and rickets.

This was the stomping ground of Mary Bateman, the Yorkshire Witch. In 1803 she poisoned three people who lived in a draper's shop near St Peter's Square in Quarry Hill and then robbed the house and shop. In 1809 she was hanged at York for the murder, by poisoning, of Rebecca Perigo, the wife of a Bramley clothier. Mary's corpse was dissected in public to raise funds for the infirmary. Her skeleton resides in the Thackray Medical Museum.

The immediate area has witnessed something of a social and cultural revolution and regeneration: apart from Quarry House it is home to the West Yorkshire Playhouse which opened in 1990, the BBC Yorkshire building, Northern Ballet and the Leeds College of Music.

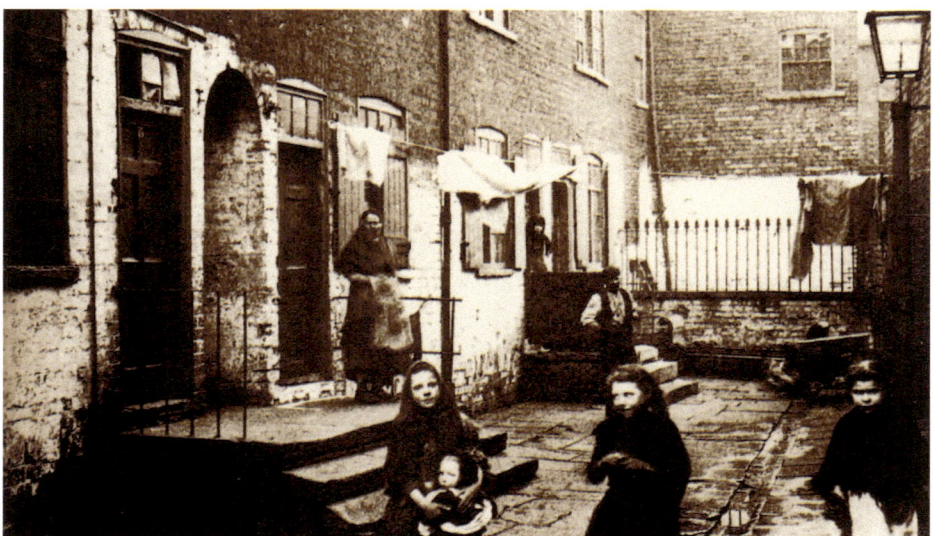

These slum conditions were prevalent throughout Leeds, and it was this that the Quarry Hill development was intended to put an end to. (Courtesy of Leodis, © Leeds Library & Information Services)

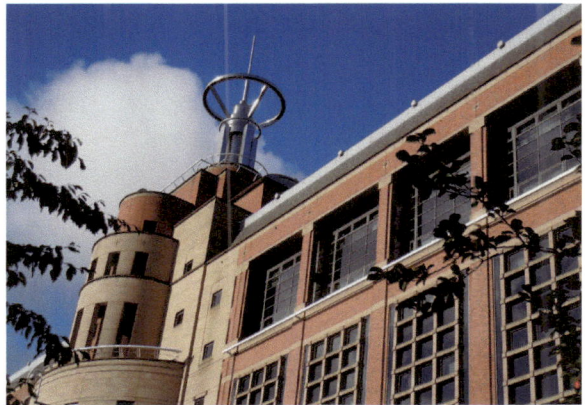

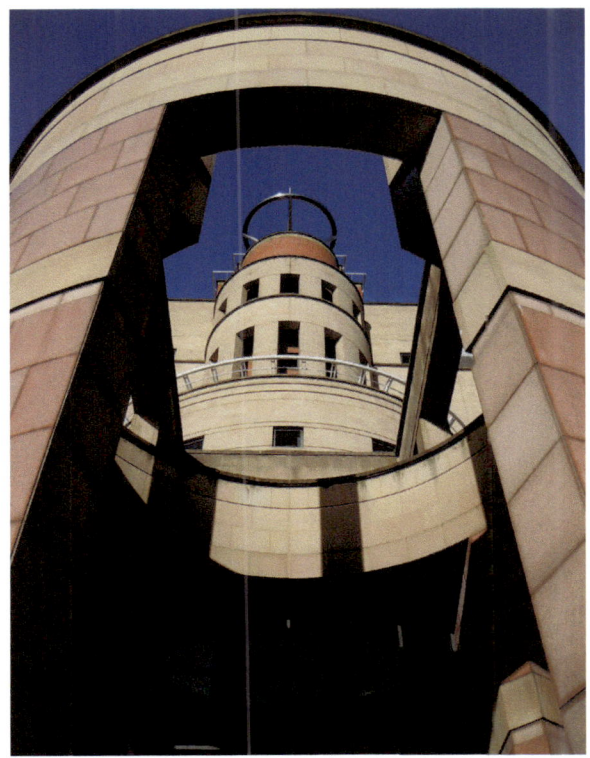

Quarry House in 2015. Its sheer bulk looms down on the eastern gateway to the city like something out of a dystopian novel.

42. Royal Armouries Museum (1996), Armouries Drive, Clarence Dock

The Royal Armouries Museum displays the National Collection of Arms and Armour and is the National Firearms Centre. It is part of the Royal Armouries family of three museums, the others being the Tower of London and Fort Nelson, near Portsmouth.

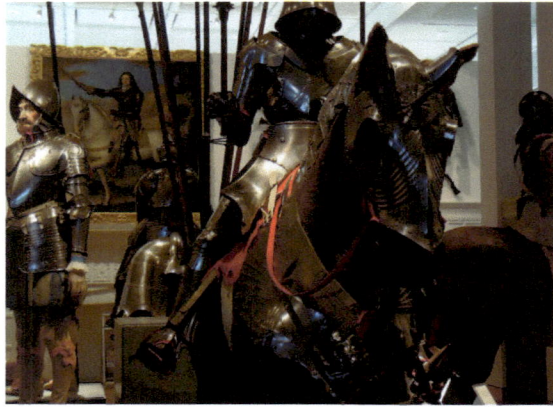

Part of the medieval display at the armouries.

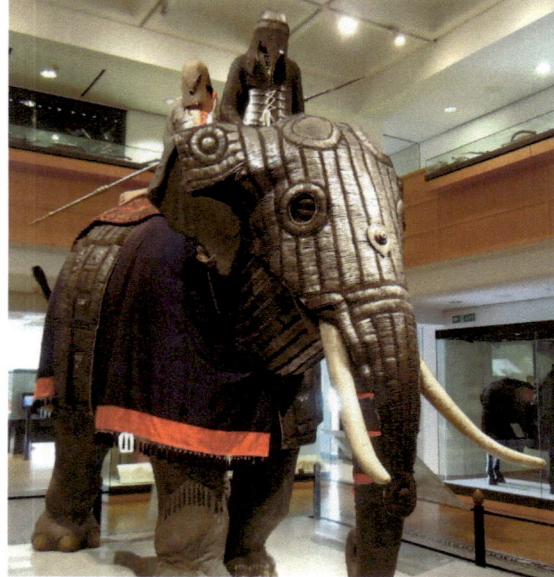

Armoured elephant – an early version of the tank, one of the first weapons of mass destruction.

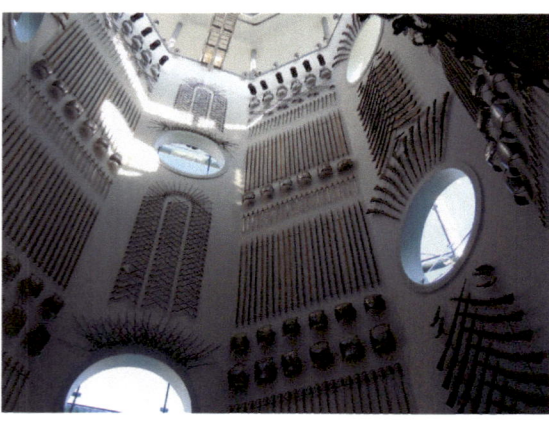

A magnificent cathedral of weaponry.

Interestingly, the museum was designed from the inside out. The design took the display spaces, together with the study collections, conservation workshops and library as the foundation of its overall layout. The ceiling heights were specifically made so that the longest weapons in the collections, displayed vertically, and the principal lift needed to move the largest object, could be accommodated comfortably.

Five galleries house 75,000 objects along with the Peace Gallery; the museum also features the Hall of Steel, a huge staircase 'whose walls are decorated with trophy displays composed of 2,500 objects reminiscent of the historical trophy displays erected by the Tower Armouries from the seventeenth century'.

The galleries include the following displays:

- Ancient and medieval warfare
- Seventeenth and eighteenth centuries
- Nineteenth and twentieth centuries
- Peace – farewell to arms? Explores the potential for a future free of arms, looking at disarmament and concepts such as détente in partnership with the Peace Museum in Bradford.
- Hunting
- Hunting through the ages
- Hunting as sport
- Oriental
- South and South-east Asia
- China and Japan

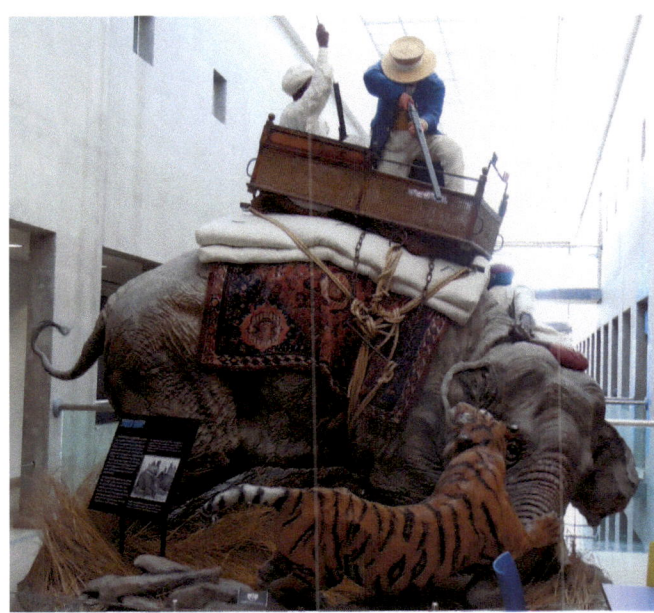

Tiger hunting by elephant.

- Central Asia, Islam and India
- Tournament
- A variety of arms and armour from the days of jousting with contests taking place from Easter.
- Self defence
- Arms and armour as art
- The armed civilian

43. Thackray Museum (1997), Beckett Street

The building now housing the fascinating Thackray Medical Museum opened in 1861 as the first purpose-built Leeds Union Workhouse to accommodate 784 paupers. Over time new buildings were added to the workhouse including a separate infirmary. By the end of the nineteenth century, the buildings were mainly used for medical care of the poor rather than traditional workhouse activity, the reason being that Leeds initially opted not to cooperate with the New Poor Law. Its Local Act status exempted it from many of the provisions of the 1834 Poor Law Amendment Act. However, in 1844 the Poor Law Commissioners placed the township's poor relief administration under a new body, the Leeds Guardians. One of the first things they did was build, in 1848, the Moral and Industrial Training Schools on the north side of Beckett Street in Leeds.

During the First World War it was called the East Leeds War Hospital, caring for armed services personnel. In 1925 the Leeds Union Workhouse infirmary was repurposed and renamed St James's Hospital; in 1945, the rest of the workhouse had merged with the hospital and it became part of the NHS in 1948. By the 1990s, the old Leeds Union Workhouse building was considered unfit for the practice of modern medicine. Permission was then given for it to house the Thackray Medical Museum, which opened in 1997.

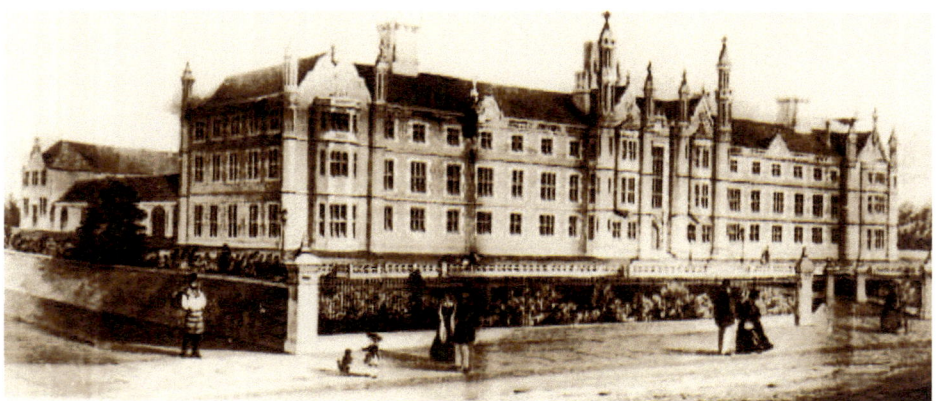

Moral and Industrial Training Schools in 1848. (© St James Hospital, Leeds)

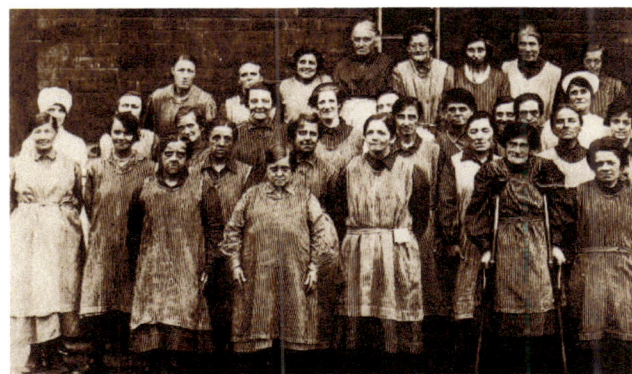

Leeds workhouse female inmates. (© St James Hospital, Leeds)

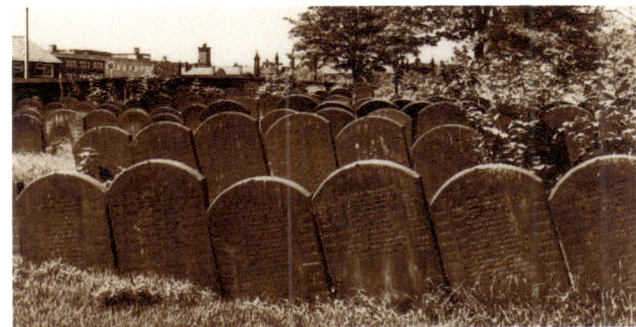

Leeds workhouse from the cemetery – the last resting place of many paupers. (© St James Hospital, Leeds)

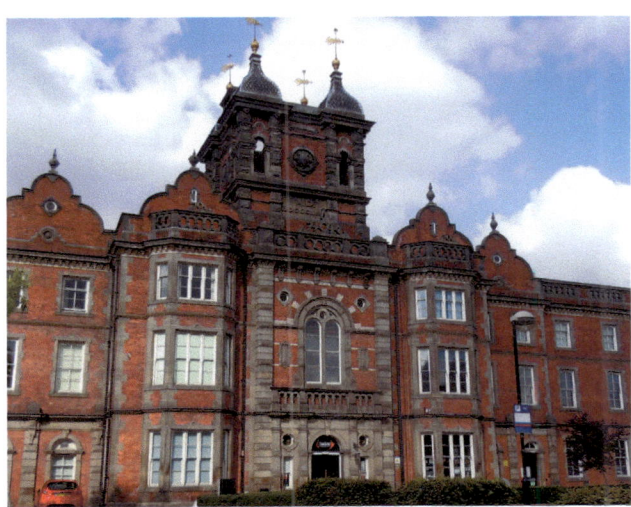

Leeds workhouse today: the Thackray Museum.

Exhibitions include 'Leeds 1842: Life in Victorian Leeds': a walk through slum streets with authentic sights, sounds and smells following the lives, illnesses and treatments of eight Victorians, making choices that determine their survival, or otherwise, among the rats, fleas and bugs. 'Pain, Pus and Blood' describes surgery before anaesthesia, and advances in pain relief and finally 'Having a Baby' focuses on developments in childbirth safety. Hannah Dyson's *Ordeal* is a video reconstruction of 1842 surgery, pre-anaesthetics – you watch as a surgeon, his assistant and a group of trainee doctors prepare for Hannah Dyson's operation, the amputation of her leg crushed in a mill accident. (The actual operation is not seen.) The 'Life Zone' is an interactive children's gallery, looking at how the human body works, with a smaller room for under fives. The museum is also home the skeleton of Mary Bateman, the 'Yorkshire Witch', who was executed for fraud and murder in 1809.

44. Leeds Makkah Masjid (2003), Thornville Road

The stunning Leeds Makkah Masjid is one of the main masjid in Leeds serving the Muslim communities of Headingley, Hyde Park, Universities and surrounding areas. The mosque suddenly appears out of the surrounding terraced streets. It arose from a dire need to accommodate the burgeoning Muslim community locally.

After much opposition from the council, planning permission was finally given to build a new mosque on the site of a dilapidated Christadelphian church which had been redundant for many years. This was a unique church constructed with a wooden structure and was a registered listed building – hence the opposition.

Leeds Makkah Masjid was finally opened on 29 August 2003 at a cost of £1.8 million – a truly magnificent response to an appeal for funds. The mosque reflects classical Arabic and Persian influences and is decorated on the outside with attractive blue, green and cream tiles. The magnificent dome inside features more calligraphy than any other mosque in the UK. It was produced by the famous Pakistani calligrapher Naveed Bhatti and comprises the ninety-nine names of Allah and Muhammad, the names of the famous companions, various verses

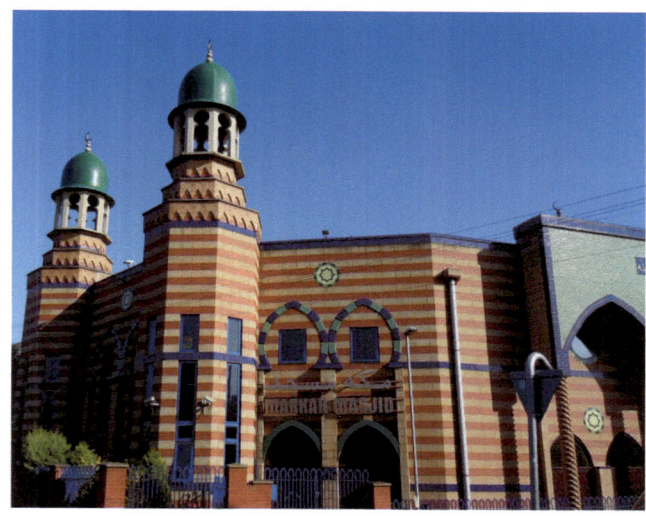

The stunning architecture of Leeds Makkah Masjid.

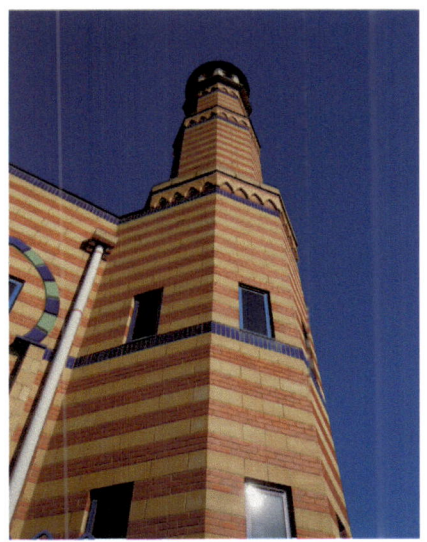

More stunning architecture at Leeds Makkah Masjid.

from the holy Quran and a complete chapter of the holy Quran (chapter 55). The mosque website (makkahmasjid.co.uk) adds:

> The calligraphy has been produced in a combination of breathtaking colours, the result of which is truly magnificent, inspiring and spiritually uplifting. The art form developed by Muslim artists, namely the art of arabesque, is also used inside the dome. Multiple coloured leaf patterns fill the inside of the dome to create a sense of a heavenly garden overlooking the congregation in prayer and meditation.

The building has three floors and can hold over 2,700 people. It has three minarets and the dome. There are two main halls for men and another for women. The mosque also has rooms for computers and a library.

45. Bridgewater Place (2005), Water Lane

Bridgewater Place, or 'the Dalek' to locals, is a prestigious office and residential skyscraper development. Not only is it the tallest building in Leeds, it is Yorkshire's tallest building by a long chalk at 112 metres (367 feet) – you can see it 25 miles away. Bridgewater Place comprises thirty-two storeys: two are car parks, ten are used for offices and twenty are residential, providing 200 flats and 400 underground car parking spaces. It is probably the only building in Yorkshire to have killed a man.

Bridgewater Place has not been without its controversies – architecturally and aesthetically, and in critical matters of wind-related public safety. 2008 saw Building Design (harshly) shortlist the building for its annual Carbuncle Cup, awarded to 'buildings so ugly they freeze the heart'. More seriously, the

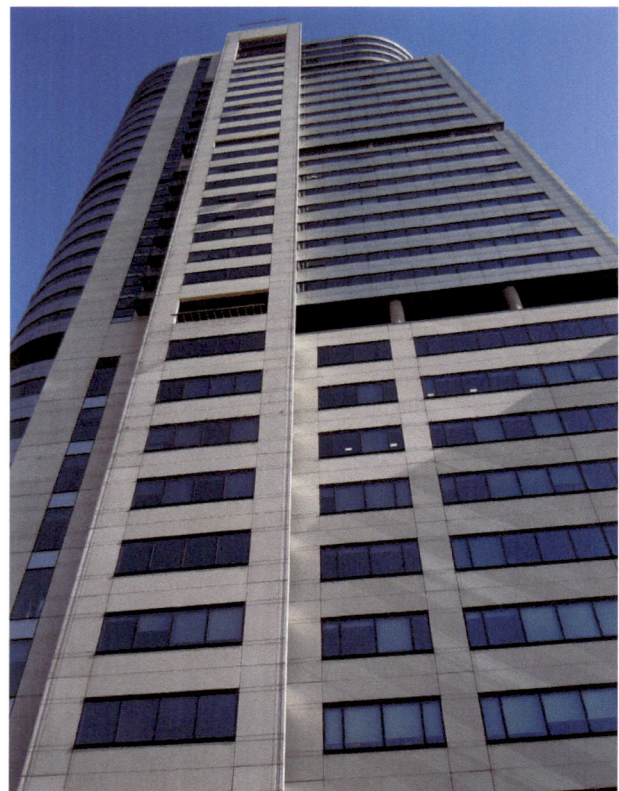

Looking up to Bridgewater Place. Yorkshire's tallest building.

design of the building accelerates winds around it – 'vortex shedding on the leeward side' from westerly winds – causing even large vehicles and pedestrians to be blown over. In March 2011 a man was killed under a lorry which had been blown over onto him. After the inquest in 2013, Leeds Deputy Coroner recommended that roads in the vicinity be closed to vehicles when wind speeds exceed 45 mph. Other schemes to mitigate the effect of the winds have been put in place.

46. Broadcasting Tower (2009), Woodhouse Lane

This is part of Leeds Beckett University, housing its Faculty of Arts, Environment and Technology, as well as some student accommodation. It is clad in COR-TEN weathering steel, which makes it look (intentionally) like it is rusting away. In 2010, Broadcasting Place was voted the Best Tall Building in the World by the Council on Tall Buildings and Urban Habitat. Other structures using COR-TEN include the Angel of the North at Gateshead. COR-TEN steel is a group of steel alloys designed to eliminate the need for painting, and form a stable rust-like appearance when exposed to the weather over time.

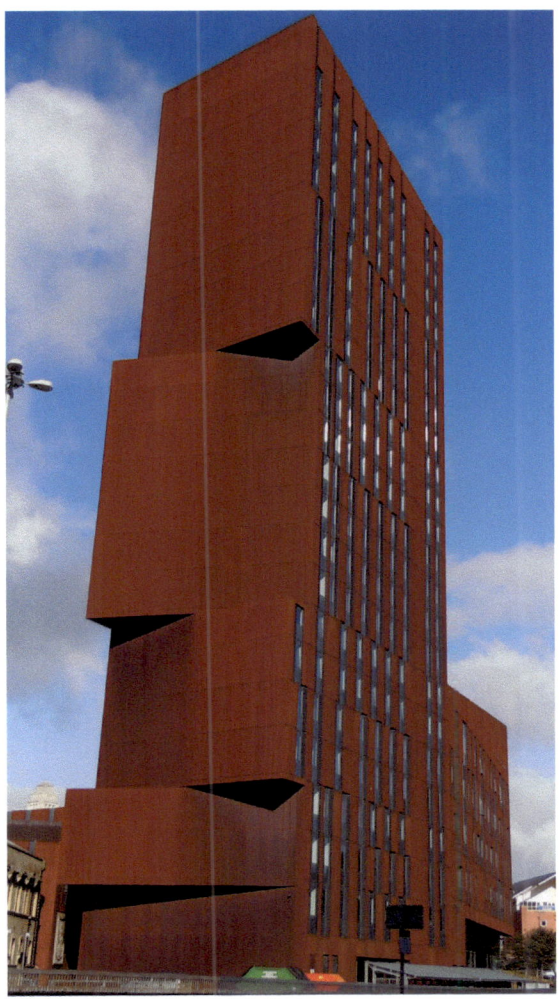

Broadcasting Tower – rusting away, deliberately.

47. Candle House (2009), Granary Wharf

Candle House is the second residential building of the proposed Granary Wharf scheme, designed by Carey Jones. The twisted cylindrical residential tower is named after the candle and tallow packing warehouses that occupied this site; the candle-like shape of the building is no accident either. The 160-apartment eco-friendly building is a twenty-three-storey cylindrical brick tower – the façade itself 'twisting' at four-storey intervals. Candle House is also intended to reference the three neighbouring Italianate towers of the Tower Works building – one of the most famous structures in Leeds. The top floor is the highest communal roof garden in Leeds; the ground floor boasts boating facilities including a restored dry dock and graving dock for boaters.

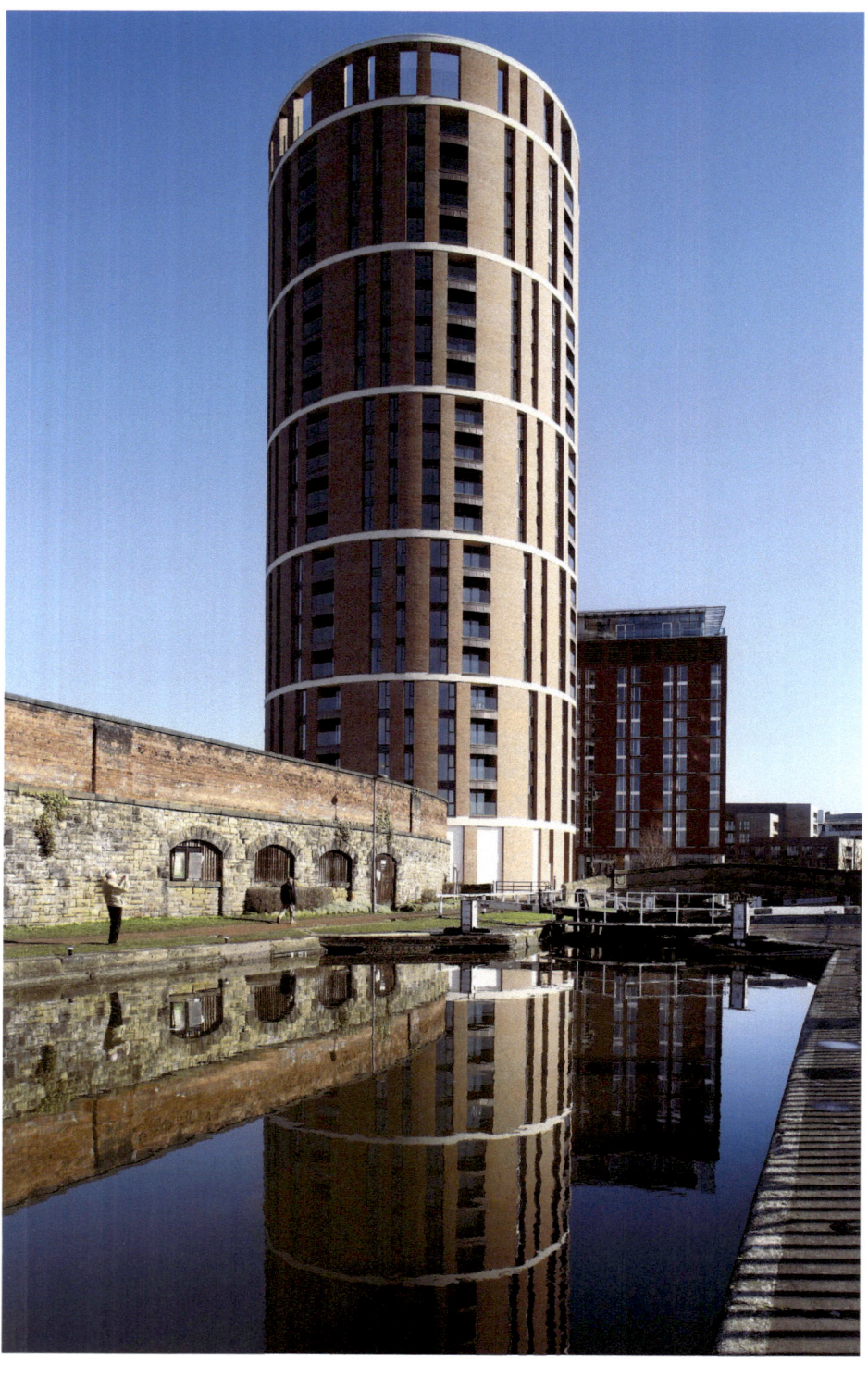

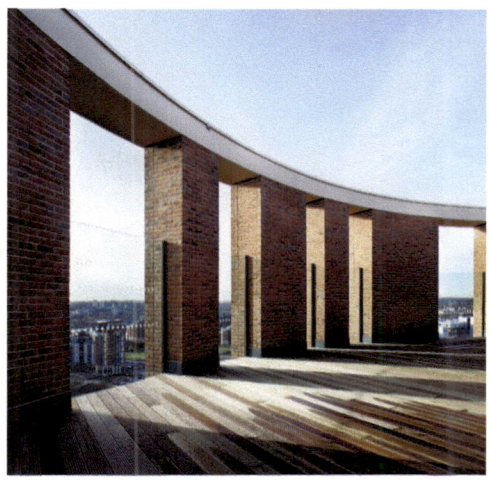

Candle Tower – from the bottom (opposite), and from the top. (Photographs courtesy of architects CJCT studios)

48. The Rose Bowl (2009), Portland Crescent

The Rose Bowl houses the Business School at Leeds Beckett University; its teaching areas and the lecture theatres are accommodated in a pod which seems to float in the space of the atrium. Being so close to the Civic Hall, the challenge was to make this twenty-first-century building fit into such an important part of the cityscape and to ensure that it was entirely sympathetic to its surroundings. According to architects Sheppard Robson,

> The scale of the new school responds to the architectural rhythm of the civic hall, clad in stone, translucent and transparent glass and pressed metal spandrel panels. The development integrates the university with the wider context of its location, orientating the campus towards Leeds city centre.

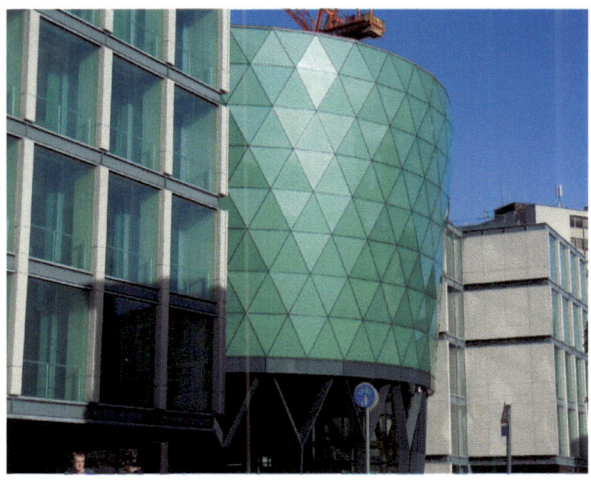

Leeds Beckett Rose Bowl.

49. Sky Plaza (2009), Clay Pit Lane

Sky Plaza, or The Plaza Tower, is a 348-foot (106 m) skyscraper comprising 572 student apartments and is the world's second tallest agglomeration of student flats, the third tallest being Prodigy Living (or Nido Spitalfields) in London. The tallest is Student Castle next to Oxford Road railway station in Manchester. While it is not the tallest building in Leeds, (Bridgewater Place is), the roof of the Plaza is the highest point in Leeds as the Plaza is built on higher ground. Like Bridgewater it can be seen from as far away as 25 miles (40 km).

Its thirty-seven storeys provide shelter for students from the University of Leeds, Leeds Beckett University and Leeds College of Music.

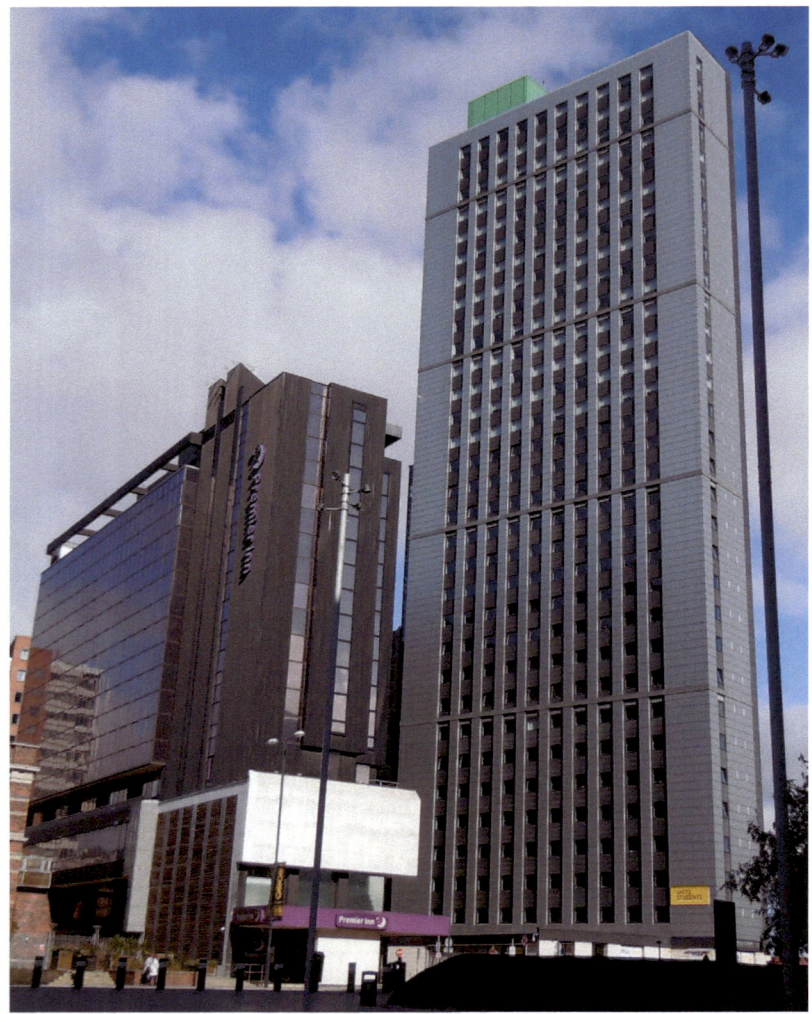

Sky Plaza in 2015.

50. First Direct Arena (2013), Clay Pit Lane

First Direct Arena is Leeds' newest major entertainment venue hosting live bands, comedy, entertainment shows and sporting events. It is the first in the United Kingdom to have a fan-shaped orientation as opposed to the more usual bowl or horseshoe seating arrangement.

In its first two years the 13,000 capacity Arena has already played host to, among others, Elton John, Bruce Springsteen (the first musician to perform there), Sports Personality of the Year, Prince, Le Tour De France Grand Départ, Queen and Adam Lambert, Eagles, Leonard Cohen, Rod Stewart, Kaiser Chiefs, Fleetwood Mac, Lionel Richie, Bette Midler, Paloma Faith, Morrissey, The MOBO Awards, and Mumford & Sons.

The arena boasts 'perfect sightlines' from every seat; the longest distance from the stage is a mere 68 metres compared with the 95–110 metres of traditionally designed arenas. According to the Arena's website 'the Arena's unique "super theatre" style configuration is designed to enhance the arena experience, with all seats facing the stage and high-quality acoustics providing the best sound experience in the UK' (firstdirectarena.com).

Furthermore, flat floor seating has been installed so that fifteen rows of retractable seating can be removed to create a huge standing area for spectators.

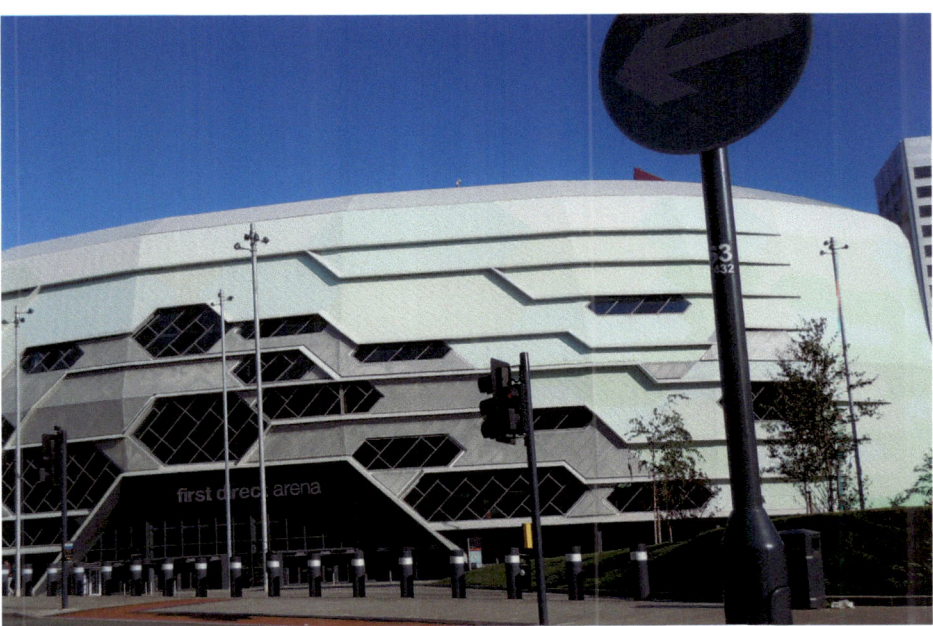

Leeds Arena – bringing Leeds as a major venue into the twenty-first century.

A Leeds Building Timeline

AD 731	Bede makes first reference to 'Loidis'
1069	Leeds escapes the Harrying of the North; Bramley, Beeston etc. devastated
1086	Leeds mentioned in Domesday Book
1152	Kirkstall Abbey founded
1155	Knights Templar take over Newsam
1185	First fulling mill in England recorded at Temple Newsam
1207	Maurice Paynel grants Leeds a charter
1258	Market operating in Leeds
1300	Leeds' population around 1,000
1322	Mention of the first bridge over the River Aire – probably one since eleventh century
1552	Leeds Grammar School established
1615	Moot Hall built in Briggate
1624	John Harrison builds new grammar school
1626	Charles I grants charter
1634	John Harrison constructs St John's church
1645	Bubonic plague kills 1,325 people
1661	Second charter grants Leeds a mayor
1684	Market moved from Leeds Bridge to Briggate
1694	George Sorocold builds water supply in Leeds
1711	New Moot Hall opened
1755	Street lighting introduced
1758	First Railway Act establishes Middleton Railway
1768	Leeds Library founded
1770	Act passes to permit Leeds and Liverpool Canal to be built
1771	Leeds Infirmary opens
1775	White Cloth Hall built in the Calls
1777	Assembly Rooms opened
1792	John Marshall moves his flax mill from Adel to Holbeck
1792	Benjamin Gott starts building his mill at Bean Ing
1812	Matthew Murray's steam engines begin operating on Middleton Railway
1816	Leeds and Liverpool Canal completed
1819	Leeds Philosophical and Literary Society established
1822	Joshua Tetley buys Sykes' Brewery

1832	Cholera epidemic in Leeds
1834	First railway from Leeds
1835	Municipal Reform Bill gives town new corporation – George Goodman
1842	Chartists 'Plug Riots' in town
1847	Typhus epidemic in Leeds
1847	Armley Jail opened
1847	First synagogue opened
1848	2,000 die in cholera epidemic
1848	Leeds Moral and Industrial Training School opened – eventually becomes St James'
1858	Queen Victoria opens town hall
1861	Corn exchange opened
1868	New Infirmary on Great George Street opened
1871	Leeds School Board formed
1871	First horse trams running
1873	Bewerley Street, the first school board purpose-built school opened
1874	Yorkshire College of Science – eventually Leeds University – opened
1874	Leeds Fine Art Club founded
1878	John Barran opens Moorish-Venetian style ready-made clothing factory in Park Square
1878	Thornton's Arcade opens
1884	Michael Marks opens stall in Leeds market
1889	Thoresby Society founded
1889	Headingley Sports Ground developed
1893	Leeds becomes a city
1898	Leeds Savage Club established in 1898 established for people interested in art, music and literature
1903	City Square opened
1904	Leeds University established
1904	New St Anne's Cathedral opened
1925	Montague Burton's is the largest and most popular clothing factory in Europe
1933	Civic Hall opened by George V
1933	BBC opens Broadcasting House on Woodhouse Lane
1959	Trams stop operating in the city
1965	Leeds Civic Trust established
1970	Leeds Polytechnic established
1978	Opera North based at the Grand Theatre
1981	Radio Aire begins broadcasting
1982	The Queen opens Henry Moore Sculpture Gallery
1990	West Yorkshire Playhouse opened

1992   Polytechnic now Leeds Metropolitan University
1997   Thackray Museum
2003   Leeds Makkah Masjid built
2005   Bridgewater Place opens as Leeds' tallest structure
2014   Leeds Arena opens

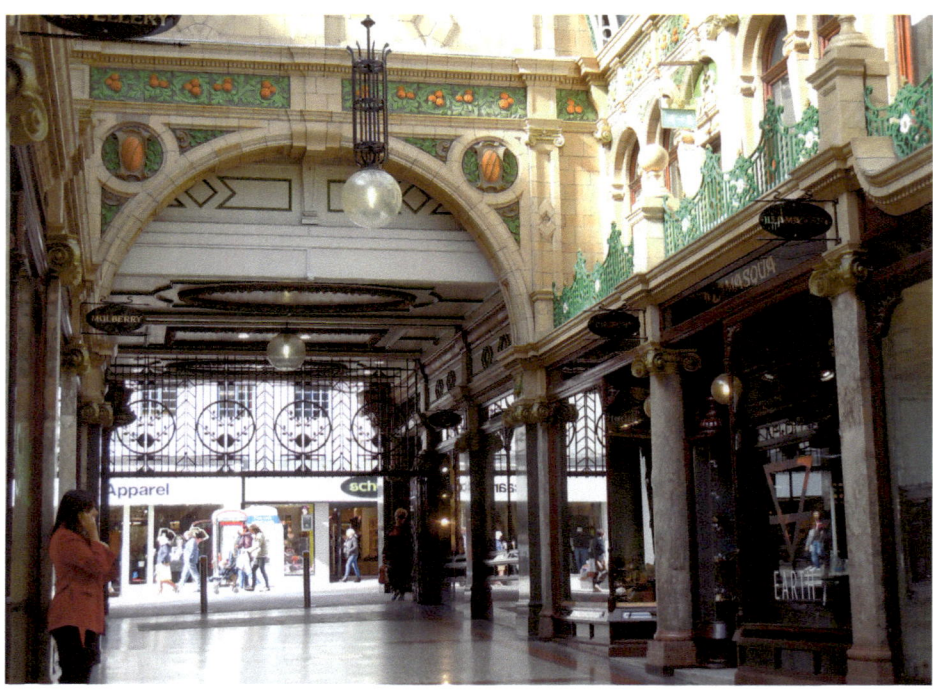

Inside the breathtaking arcades in 2015.

Websites

http://www.thoresby.org.uk/library.htm
http://www.aireboroughcivicsociety.org.uk/
http://www.nationalarchives.gov.uk/a2a/
http://www.leeds.ac.uk/heritage/
http://www.leeds.ac.uk/ims/about/events.html
http://www.yas.org.uk/
http://www.archives.wyjs.org.uk/
http://www.elhas.org.uk/
http://www.ancestry.com/
http://www.barwickinelmethistoricalsociety.com/
http://www.cix.co.uk/~archaeology/cia/index.htm
http://www.leodis.net/
http://www.yfaonline.com/yfapublic/index.cfm
http://www.gravestonephotos.com/
http://tithemaps.leeds.gov.uk/TwinMaps.aspx
http://www.bigbookend.co.uk/category/blog/leeds-history/

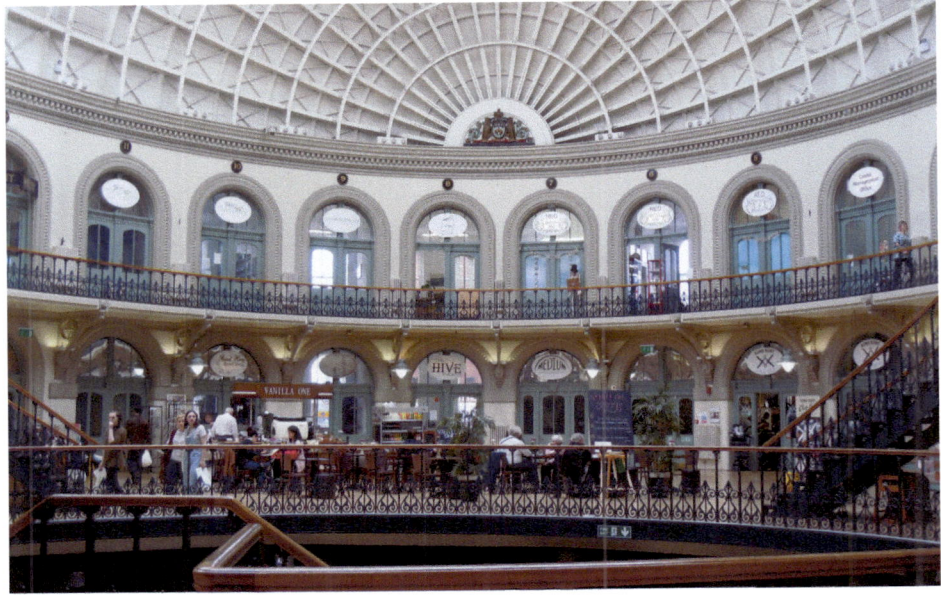

Inside the corn market in 2015.

Acknowledgements

The people of Leeds have been extraordinarily supportive and generous in the help they have given me towards the compilation of this book. Without them the book would be considerably less informative and significantly less colourful. I would, therefore, like to thank the following for their assistance in the provision of information and of some stunning photography.

They are Jim Albentosa at the Warehouse; Anys Williams at Anita Morris Associates for the Corn Exchange images; Susan Williamson at Temple Works; Sally Hughes, Assistant Librarian Manager, Local and Family History Library, Leeds Central Library for the Leodis images; Geoff Munitz, Jewish Genealogical Society of Great Britain; Peter Higginbotham at workhouses.org.uk; Laura Keenan at CJCT Studios for the pictures of Candle House; Ollie Jenkins, Picture House Administrator, Hyde Park Picture House; Andrew Bannister, Head of Media Relations and Leeds Teaching Hospitals NHS Trust.

Related books by the same author:

Harrogate Pubs
Secret Harrogate
Harrogate Through Time
Knaresborough Through Time
Vale of York Through Time
Confectionery in Yorkshire
Secret Knaresborough
Changing Scarborough
Secret York
Tea: A Very British Beverage
Coffee: A Drink for the Devil
Tadcaster Through Time
Chocolate

For a full list please go to www.paulchrystal.com.
Unless acknowledged otherwise all photography is © Paul Chrystal.